Exploring the Shape of Space

Jeffrey R. Weeks

Key Curriculum Press
Innovators in Mathematics Education

Project Editor: Joan Lewis
Editorial Assistant: Heather Dever
Software Development: Jeffrey R. Weeks
Teacher Reviewer: Kay Shager
Mathematics Reviewer: Larry Copes
Science Reviewer: Sheldon Carroll
Production Editor: Kristin Ferraioli
Copy Editor: Mary Roybal
Production and Manufacturing Manager: Diana Jean Parks
Text Designer and Production Coordinator: Jenny Somerville
Compositor: Christi Payne, Book Arts
Art Editor: Jason Luz
Technical Artist: Tom Webster, Lineworks, Inc.
Illustrator and Photo Researcher: Jason Luz
Art and Design Coordinator: Caroline Ayres
Cover Designer: Jenny Somerville
Prepress and Printing: Versa Press, Inc.

Executive Editor: Casey FitzSimons
Publisher: Steven Rasmussen

© 2001 by Key Curriculum Press. All rights reserved.

Limited Reproduction Permission
The publisher grants the teacher who purchases *Exploring the Shape of Space* the right to reproduce material for use in his or her own classroom. Unauthorized copying of *Exploring the Shape of Space* constitutes copyright infringement and is a violation of federal law.

The material is based upon work supported by the National Science Foundation under awards ESI-9550493 (Torus and Klein Bottle Games), DMS89-20161 (*The Shape of Space* video), and ESI-9730250 (classroom materials). Any opinions, findings, and conclusions or recommendations expressed in this publication are those of the author and do not necessarily reflect the views of the National Science Foundation.

Key Curriculum Press
1150 65th Street
Emeryville, CA 94608
510-595-7000
editorial@keypress.com
http://www.keypress.com

Printed in the United States of America
10 9 8 7 6 5 4 3 2 1   04 03 02 01 00
ISBN 1-55953-467-2

Acknowledgments

A great many people contributed to these materials.

First and foremost, the participants in the 1998 *Shape of Space in the Middle School* workshop brought the materials into classroom-ready form. They spent the first week of the workshop revising the materials for classroom use, and then spent the second week testing them with a group of middle school students (grades 6 and 7) and making additional revisions. In the fall of 1998, workshop participants piloted the resulting unit with their own classes (grades 3 through 10), and suggested further improvements. The practicality of the final unit is the result of their efforts and imagination. The workshop participants were Matt Bardoe, Creative Children's Academy; Kerry Hanifl, Apple Valley High School; Mike Huberty, Mounds View High School; Robin Jones, Breck School; and Monica Kocourek, Benilde–St. Margaret's School. Lori Thomson of The Geometry Center played a key role, both in the creation of the materials and as a co-organizer of the workshop. Arnie Cutler, Linda Halet, and Dick McGehee handled many of the behind-the-scenes arrangements.

The Torus and Klein Bottle Games on which the unit depends were developed as part of the Space Explorations Project at Bolt, Beranek, and Newman, for teaching visual mathematics at the high school level. Gabriel Katz and Wally Feurzeig led that project. Most importantly, Wally Feurzeig had the inspiration to develop separate curriculum materials suitable for middle school. Phil Lewis also provided useful ideas.

The other multimedia component of the unit, the video *The Shape of Space,* was produced at The Geometry Center in 1995 by Charlie Gunn, Stuart Levy, Delle Maxwell, Tamara Munzner, Lori Thomson, and Jeff Weeks.

In the summer of 1995, a team at The Geometry Center produced a comprehensive set of teaching materials for the shape of space concept and related ideas in topology and geometry. The team members were Barbara Foster, James Huber, Laura Moss, Jodi Schneider, Jerald TerEick, and Daniel Verinder. Chaim Goodman-Strauss advised them.

In the spring of 1997, Lori Thomson produced a set of Web-based classroom materials to support the video *The Shape of Space,* drawing on the work of the 1995 summer team. The present unit, in turn, incorporates parts of Lori's work.

Independently of The Geometry Center, Dan Stromgren and Rick Tomlinson (McKenney Middle School, Canton NY) let me pilot early versions of this unit with their students and provided excellent suggestions for improving the materials. Lori Thomson collaborated in preparing the materials for those classes.

The anonymous reviewers for the National Science Foundation and, especially, Alverna Champion helped shape this project, and provided help and encouragement in getting it out into the schools where it can enrich children's lives. I thank the NSF for funding the main development of these materials, and the John D. and Catherine T. MacArthur Foundation for its support during later revisions.

Finally, Joan Lewis, Kristin Ferraioli, Jason Luz, Jenny Somerville, and their colleagues at Key Curriculum Press guided these lessons into their final form.

Jeff Weeks

Contents

    To the Teacher … vii
    Why Explore the Shape of Space? … ix
    How to Use This Book … xi
    Resources … xiii

1 Flatland … 1
    Teacher Notes … 2
    Transparency 1: How Big Is the Universe? … 5
    Activity 1: How Big Is the Universe? … 6
    Homework 1: Flatland … 7

2 Wraparound Universe … 9
    Teacher Notes … 10
    Transparency 2: Definitions … 13
    Activity 2a: Coordinates … 14
    Activity 2b: Dimensions … 16
    Activity 2c: Finite/Infinite, Boundary/No Boundary … 18
    Homework 2: Wraparound Universe … 20

3 Cylindrical Tic-Tac-Toe … 23
    Teacher Notes … 24
    Transparency 3: Tic-Tac-Toe … 28
    Activity 3a: Tic-Tac-Toe on a Cylinder … 29
    Activity 3b: Equivalent Games … 30
    Homework 3: Cylindrical Tic-Tac-Toe … 31

4 Torus Games … 33
    Teacher Notes … 34
    Transparency 4: Torus Introduction … 37
    Homework 4: Torus Games … 38

5 More Torus Games … 41
    Teacher Notes … 42
    Transparency 5: Tiling View Introduction … 44
    Activity 5: Games on a Torus … 45
    Homework 5: More Torus Games … 48

6 The 3-Torus — 51
Teacher Notes — 52
Video Guide 1: *The Shape of Space*, Part 1 — 55
Transparency 6: The Real Universe — 56
Activity 6a: The Real Universe — 57
Activity 6b: Torus Dimensions — 58
Homework 6: The 3-Torus — 61
Reading: Cosmology — 63
Celestial Map: Locating the Andromeda Galaxy — 68

7 Möbius Strips — 69
Teacher Notes — 70
Transparency 7a: Möbius Tic-Tac-Toe — 72
Transparency 7b: Tic-Tac-Toe Tiling View — 73
Activity 7a: Making Möbius Strips — 74
Activity 7b: Möbius Strip Tiling View — 76
Homework 7: Möbius Strips — 78

8 Klein Bottle Games — 81
Teacher Notes — 82
Transparency 8: Klein Bottle Games Introduction — 85
Activity 8: Games on a Klein Bottle — 86
Homework 8: Klein Bottle Games — 88

9 More Shapes for Space — 91
Teacher Notes — 92
Video Guide 2: *The Shape of Space*, Part 2 — 96
Activity 9: Mystery Spaces — 97
Homework 9: More Shapes for Space — 102

Test — 103

Answers — 107

Glossary — 129

To the Teacher

The seed from which this unit sprouted was an early version of the Torus and Klein Bottle Games. The games were intended to let high school and college students learn about different spaces by playing games in them. I was pleasantly surprised to discover that my son (then four years old) and his friends had no problems playing these games in strange spaces. I soon realized that the difficulties adults experience when learning new concepts of space aren't so much with the new ideas themselves, but with unlearning their old ways of thinking. Children approach new ideas with open minds and fewer old ideas to overcome.

It was also clear that children learn geometry by seeing and doing, not by listening or reading. In other words, as they concentrate on their strategy in a torus tic-tac-toe game or lead a mouse through a Klein bottle maze to reach the cheese, children build up an intuition for the new kind of space in which the tic-tac-toe board or maze exists.

Over the next few years the video *The Shape of Space* video supplemented the games, and the classroom activities completed the package. I hope you and your students have as much fun with these materials as my students and I have had. If, when looking up at the sky on a clear night, your students see the universe as they've never seen it before, this unit will have been a success.

Jeff Weeks
Canton, New York
September 2000

Why Explore the Shape of Space?

Why should you teach *Exploring the Shape of Space* in your classes? There are three reasons:

Mathematical reason

Exploring the Shape of Space provides a solid introduction to 1-, 2-, and 3-dimensional geometry for students in grades six through ten. One teacher, Robin Jones, taught the unit in September as the first topic in her sixth-grade mathematics classes, and commented

> One thing I have noticed since ending the unit is that my students' understanding of one, two, and three dimensions has held. When we talk about area and volume, they're much more knowledgeable than the kids I taught last year. They have learned to visualize better.

Students at all levels will see that geometry is a living subject responding to the needs of twenty-first century science, not a dead discipline finalized in ancient times. The unit supports the *Principles and Standards for School Mathematics* set forth by the National Council of Teachers of Mathematics and places a strong emphasis on creative problem solving and the tight connections between the geometry and its cosmological applications.

Social reason

The middle school mathematics curriculum often becomes stratified. Brighter students enjoy a wealth of enrichment activities, while average students are left with a numbing repetition of decimals, fractions, and percents. Mastery of decimals, fractions, and percents is of course essential, but average students also need to stretch their minds with new and beautiful ideas. *Exploring the Shape of Space* is ideal for this purpose. The main idea (that space can be finite yet have no boundary) is new and startling, yet elegantly simple. Best of all, it makes its demands on the students' imaginations, not their computational abilities, so the unit appeals to and is accessible to all students, independently of their previous success in mathematics. (Classroom testing has borne this claim out. A sixth-grade teacher who taught the unit simultaneously to her one gifted class, two average classes, and one remedial class reported that while the gifted class did better on the exam, the students in the remedial class did as well as those in the average class.) The unit sparks the interest of students at risk of being turned off by mathematics. In particular, the unit reaches visual learners who often struggle with the standard middle school curriculum.

Scientific reason

Humanity may soon answer the ancient question of whether the universe is finite or infinite, using data from satellites to be launched by NASA in 2001 and the European Space Agency in 2007. (For details, please see the Cosmology reading on page 63.) *Exploring the Shape of Space* prepares students to appreciate these experiments by letting them see how the universe can be finite yet have no boundary, and by helping them develop an intuitive understanding of several possible shapes.

How to Use This Book

Exploring the Shape of Space introduces students to one, two, and three dimensions in a very modern way, by exploring some possible shapes for our 3-dimensional universe. The students learn by example, using paper-and-scissors activities, pencil-and-paper games, Java-based computer games, and a computer-animated video (*The Shape of Space*) to explore a few of the simplest possible universes in an intuitive, hands-on way. Throughout the unit, geometry interweaves with cosmology, including current research efforts to determine the shape of the real universe.

The unit contains nine lessons, including complete teacher notes, blackline master student activity sheets and homework assignments, optional transparency masters, a final test, a reproducible glossary, and an answer key. Each lesson requires one class period, with the exception that teachers of younger middle school classes may want to allow extra time in Lesson 2 for the introductory activities on coordinates. Thus, allowing one day for the test at the end, the entire unit requires ten or eleven class periods. Teachers wishing a shorter unit can do Lessons 1 through 6, omitting Lessons 7 through 9 and the test. Teachers with more time or those on block schedules can explore student ideas in greater depth during class discussions, perhaps spreading two lessons over three class periods. An extra period can be devoted to discussing the Cosmology reading in depth. As part of a longer unit, students can delve more deeply into cosmology, investigating topics such as those in the Further Study section of the Lesson 6 teacher notes. After researching their topics in a traditional library or on the Internet, students can present their results as classroom presentations, written reports, posters, or Web pages.

The lessons are a combination of whole-class discussions and activities for groups of three or four students each. The whole-class discussions appear as dialogs in the teacher notes. The dialogs needn't be followed literally, but serve to indicate the main points of the discussion in a format that's easy to glance at during class. Follow your students' interests in the discussion and realize that it sometimes takes time to arrive at the ideas you are seeking.

Lessons 1, 2, 3, 6, 7, and 9 take place in the classroom and require only the materials listed on the opening page of each lesson. Lessons 6 and 9 use the video *The Shape of Space,* sold separately in VHS or PAL format. The video is also provided in digital format on the CD-ROM included with this book. Following *The Shape of Space,* the editors have included on the same tape a short interview that PBS did with me for the series *Life by the Numbers*. To give students a view of the human side of mathematics, you may want to show the interview during the last 15 minutes of class the day you give the test.

Lessons 4, 5, and 8 require computers, either in the classroom or in a computer lab. One computer for every two students is ideal, but if computer availability is limited, one computer for every three or four students is also fine. Before you begin class, you or your school's computer specialist should copy the Torus Games folder (included on the CD-ROM in the Space folder) onto the computers' hard drives, or onto a central file server. The games are arranged on Web pages, and require a Java-capable Web browser. (Internet Explorer runs Java applets more reliably than Netscape Navigator. For more details, please see **TorusGames/html/UsingGames.html** on the CD-ROM.) When you first install the games, make a bookmark for them in each Web browser—this will save class time later by making it easy for students to locate the games quickly. Students with access to a computer after school can access the games online through Key Curriculum Press's *Exploring the Shape of Space* Web site at **http://www.keypress.com/space/.** You may also visit this Web site for

- technical support
- answers to mathematical questions that may arise
- up-to-date information on ongoing cosmological research
- new or updated software that may become available
- questions or comments for the author

Resources

1. Abbott, Edwin. *Flatland: A Romance of Many Dimensions,* New York: Dover, 1992.

   Students who enjoy the 2-dimensional worlds in Lesson 1 will love Edwin Abbott's 1884 classic *Flatland*. The first half of the book is Victorian social satire—reassure the students that Abbott was a satirist, not a misogynist! The second half gets into the geometry, chronicling the adventures of a flatlander trying to understand the third dimension, and starting the reader on the path to a fourth dimension.

   Older middle school students with good reading skills will do fine with this book, but younger students may have trouble with the nineteenth century prose. The writing is clear and powerful, but relies on an extensive vocabulary.

   This wonderful book is so inexpensive, you can buy an individual copy for every student in your class for less than the cost of a single copy of most other books.

2. Osserman, Robert. *Poetry of Universe,* New York: Anchor Books, 1996.

   An excellent historical account of the science and mathematics of the universe.

   This is truly a layperson's account—no science or mathematics background is needed—but nevertheless the book is intended mainly for adults.

3. Weeks, Jeffrey R. *The Shape of Space,* New York: Marcel Dekker, Inc., 1985.

   A complete yet elementary treatment of the mathematical ideas introduced in this unit, as well as related ideas such as curvature.

   While no specific mathematics background is required, the reader should be comfortable with the mathematical way of thinking and should enjoy solving puzzles. Strong high school mathematics students can read this book on their own, but few middle school students could.

Objectives

- To know how large the visible universe is and how many stars and galaxies it contains but to realize that, in spite of its enormous size, the universe might not be infinite.
- To understand how a 2-dimensional universe would differ from our 3-dimensional one.

1 Flatland

Materials

Transparency 1: How Big Is the Universe? (replaces Activity 1)

Activity 1: How Big Is the Universe? (one per group)

Homework 1: Flatland

Outline

Location: classroom

20 minutes: How Big Is the Universe? (whole class discussion; Activity 1)

30 minutes: Flatland (whole class)

Vocabulary

infinite

finite

boundary

2-dimensional

3-dimensional

Teacher Notes

Activities

How Big Is the Universe?

The class discussion about the size of the universe might go something like this:

How big is the universe?

Let students share their ideas. Eventually, though, all should realize that the universe is very, very big.

Are stars spread evenly throughout the universe?

No, they are grouped into galaxies. The galaxy we are in is called the Milky Way.

Guess how many stars a typical galaxy such as our Milky Way contains.

Students might guess a thousand.

More than that—guess again!

Let students keep guessing until they reach the correct answer of about a hundred billion (not million!) stars.

Guess how many galaxies are visible in the sky using a telescope.

Let students keep guessing until they reach the correct answer of about a hundred billion galaxies.

You can have students complete Activity 1 in small groups. They can use their own paper, so one copy of the activity is enough for each group. Alternatively, you can show the questions on the overhead using Transparency 1 or copy them onto the board. After students have written their answers, reconvene the class for discussion.

Keep the discussion open and follow your students' leads. It sometimes takes patience to arrive at the destination. As words from the vocabulary list are used, write them on the board. You can also bring up this argument if your students do not:

An old argument that space must be *infinite* goes like this: If space were *finite*, then it would have some sort of edge or *boundary*. But a boundary doesn't make sense, because what would happen if you traveled to the boundary of space and stuck your hand through?

People were assuming that if space has no boundary, it must be infinite. But that's not true. As we explore the shape of space, we are going to make model universes that have no boundary but are finite.

Mathematicians and cosmologists are currently very interested in such models, because the real universe may be finite. Satellite data that is to become available in the years 2001 to 2009 may reveal which model fits the real universe.

Teacher Notes

What's a cosmologist?

A scientist who studies the universe. **Cosmologist** *comes from the Greek word* kosmos, *meaning universe.*

In Lessons 4 and 5, we'll study *2-dimensional* **universes that are finite and have no boundary. When we understand the main ideas in two dimensions, we'll go on to construct finite** *3-dimensional* **spaces with no boundary in Lesson 6.**

Up-to-date information on cosmology research will be posted at http://www.keypress.com/space/.

Flatland

Talking about flatland will help students abstract the concept of dimension apart from the many other details of everyday life. Encourage students to create people, planets, and other flatland images that correspond to our world as closely as possible—but in two dimensions instead of three! Students have much fun and many laughs with this exercise.

The chalkboard makes a nice 2-dimensional universe. Can someone please come to the board and draw on it a 2-dimensional person—a "flatlander"?

(Reassure the student approaching the board that the drawing doesn't have to be perfect—it's just a starting point.)

The most common mistake people make with their first attempt at drawing a flatlander is placing the eyes on the inside of the head. This is incorrect because no light can reach the eyes—the skull and brain block it.

How will the flatlander see another flatlander?

Let students revise the drawing. The eyes should be at one edge of the head, with access to the outside world, just as we 3-dimensional humans have eyes at the edges of our heads, with access to the outside world.

The students may also mistakenly draw the mouth on the inside of the head.

How will the flatlander eat?

More revision is necessary. Just as a human's 3-dimensional mouth is an opening through which food enters the body from the outside, the flatlander's mouth should be an opening through which food enters its body from the 2-dimensional world. A reasonable final attempt at a flatlander head might look something like the figure shown at right.

Exploring the Shape of Space   **Flatland**

Teacher Notes

Emphasize the difference between a true 2-dimensional being and a 2-dimensional image of a 3-dimensional being. Keep the discussion open and let the students pursue their own ideas. Here are some questions you can ask:

Where is the flatlander's skin?

The skin is the 1-dimensional perimeter of the flatlander's 2-dimensional body, just as our skin is the 2-dimensional surface of our 3-dimensional bodies. In each case, the skin is the boundary between the inside and the outside.

How does the flatlander eat and digest food?

One particularly unsettling question is whether the digestive tract splits a flatlander's body into two pieces. Various solutions are possible. Let the students think about it, but don't worry if they don't reach a solution.

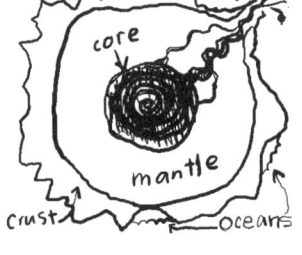

Can someone come to the board and draw a 2-dimensional planet? Please include mountains and oceans.

The mountains and oceans should be features on the planet's 1-dimensional circumference, so the drawing will look very different from a standard picture of Earth.

What goes in the middle of the planet?

If students make an analogy with Earth, they might mention magma, or core and mantle.

Could someone please come to the board and draw a close-up view of a lake between two mountains, a flatlander in a sailboat on the lake—think carefully about that sail—and a different flatlander swimming in the lake?

Does the flatlander who is swimming get wet?

Yes, where the curve that is his skin touches the water.

Can he see his friend in the boat?

No, the sail is in the way.

Homework

Distribute Homework 1, due tomorrow.

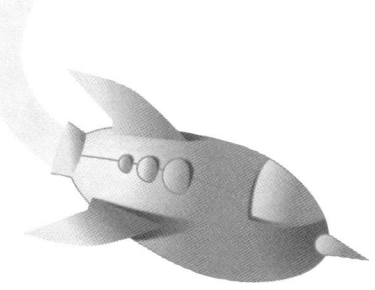

How Big Is the Universe?

1. A typical galaxy contains roughly one hundred billion stars. Write one hundred billion as a numeral.

2. Each of the roughly one hundred billion galaxies visible with the Hubble Space Telescope contains roughly one hundred billion stars. How many stars does that make altogether? Write your answer as a numeral. (How might you write your answer in words?)

3. Do you think space is infinite or finite? Why?

Activity 1

How Big Is the Universe?

Stars are not spread evenly throughout the universe but are grouped into clumps called galaxies.

1. A typical galaxy contains roughly one hundred billion stars. Write one hundred billion as a numeral.

Our sun lies in the Milky Way galaxy. All the stars you see at night are part of the Milky Way. The Andromeda galaxy, which you can see as a small white smudge in the direction of the constellation Andromeda, is the only other galaxy visible to the naked eye. But using the Hubble Space Telescope, we can see roughly one hundred billion other galaxies.

2. Each of the roughly one hundred billion galaxies visible with the Hubble Space Telescope contains roughly one hundred billion stars. How many stars does that make altogether? Write your answer as a numeral. (How might you write your answer in words?)

The universe is very, very big. But is it truly infinite? Or might there be a limit to the number of galaxies and a limit to the total volume of space? In other words, might space be finite? The words *infinite* and *finite* are antonyms.

> A universe is *infinite* if it has unlimited volume.
> A universe is *finite* if it has a limited, measurable volume.

3. Do you think space is infinite or finite? Why?

Homework 1   Name _____

Flatland

1. Draw a flatlander on the back of this page. Show details such as eyes, mouth, digestive system, arms, or legs.

2. We humans are 3-dimensional, but we see a 2-dimensional image of our world, like the image on a movie screen. Draw an image of a hockey puck first as seen from above and then as seen from the side.

　
　
　
　
　

    from above   from the side

3. What do flatlanders see? Draw a flatlander first as we humans see her from outside flatland and then as another flatlander would see her from within flatland.

　
　
　
　
　

    our view (from outside flatland)   flatlander's view (from within flatland)

Exploring the Shape of Space
©2001 Key Curriculum Press

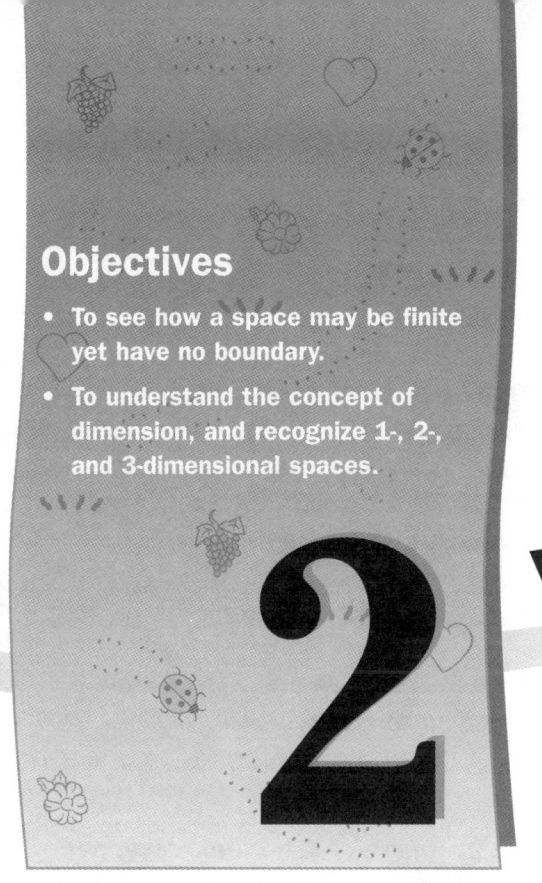

Objectives

- To see how a space may be finite yet have no boundary.
- To understand the concept of dimension, and recognize 1-, 2-, and 3-dimensional spaces.

Wraparound Universe

Materials

Graph paper or plain paper (one sheet per student)

Transparency 2: Definitions (optional)

Activity 2a: Coordinates (younger grades only)

Activity 2b: Dimensions

Activity 2c: Finite/Infinite, Boundary/No Boundary

Homework 2: Wraparound Universe

Outline

Location: classroom

20 minutes: Coordinates (Activity 2a, younger grades only)

10 minutes: Dimensions (Activity 2b, groups)

10 minutes: Wraparound Universe (whole class)

5 minutes: Lineland (whole class)

20 minutes: Finite/Infinite, Boundary/No Boundary (Activity 2c; groups)

Vocabulary

infinite

finite

boundary

1-dimensional

2-dimensional

3-dimensional

Teacher Notes

Activities

Coordinates

If your students have not studied coordinates, they will need experience in using two numbers (or a number and a letter) to locate a point on a surface. Students can identify regions of the map from the numbers and letters on the sides, or they can do Activity 2a and use latitude and longitude to locate cities on the globe's surface. To complete Question 3 on Activity 2a, the class needs to agree ahead of time on what units to use. Meters, feet, and paces are all good possibilities.

Dimensions

Have students complete Activity 2b in small groups. When they reconvene to discuss their answers, you might want to use Transparency 2. You can also present additional information about color vision.

The 3-dimensionality of color is a property of the human eye, not the external world. Our eyes have three types of color receptors, called cones. Each of the three types of cones responds to light of certain wavelengths. The intensity with which the three types of cones are stimulated determines the subjective color we perceive.

During the night, however, our eyes use different receptors, called rods. Unlike cones, rods respond well to low levels of light. But we have only one type of rod, not three, so our night vision sees only a *1-dimensional* set of colors, which we perceive as varying shades of gray.

Here are some questions to get students thinking:

Super Bonus Question 1: Some individuals lack the gene responsible for one of the three types of cones. How does this affect the set of colors they see?

> *Such individuals have only two types of cones, and therefore they see only a 2-dimensional set of colors. In its most common form, this results in red-green color blindness. Such individuals can specify any color they perceive by using only two numbers, for example, the numbers representing the intensities of red light and blue light.*

Super Bonus Question 2: New World monkeys and many species of birds—budgerigar, canary, zebra finch, mallard duck, pigeon—have four types of cones. How does this affect their color vision?

> *These birds and monkeys see a 4-dimensional set of colors. In other words, they see more colors than we do. Two colored lights that look*

identical to humans can look very different to these birds and monkeys. We cannot hope to imagine their subjective impression of this 4-dimensional set of colors, because the "extra" colors do not correspond to anything we experience. (Similarly, a person with red-green color blindness cannot hope to imagine the colors people with trichromatic vision see. Indeed, we cannot be sure that different people with trichromatic vision have the same subjective impression of the colors they see, even though they always agree about whether or not two colors are the same.)

Imagine the rich artistic possibilities open to a civilization with 4-dimensional color vision!

Wraparound Universe

Give each student a sheet of graph paper, and ask him or her to draw several flatlanders. (Plain white paper will also do, but graph paper better suggests coordinates and dimension.)

How many numbers are required to locate a point on the paper?

Two.

How many dimensions does the surface of the paper have?

It is 2-dimensional.

Challenge the students to use their paper to construct a universe in which the flatlanders can travel in a straight line and return to their starting point. Remember, it sometimes takes patience to let students arrive at an answer. Eventually, someone should suggest wrapping the paper around to make a cylinder.

How many numbers are required to locate a point on the surface of the cylinder?

Two.

How many dimensions does this cylindrical universe have?

It is 2-dimensional. Indeed, all flatlander universes must be 2-dimensional.

Lineland

Our universe is 3-dimensional, and flatland is 2-dimensional. What might a 1-dimensional space be?

A line.

Could someone please come to the board and draw some linelanders?

Teacher Notes

Linelanders should be a part of the line. Students might incorrectly draw a flatlander walking on the line, the way a tightrope walker walks on a rope. If so, remind them that the linelanders should be 1-dimensional and should live entirely within their 1-dimensional universe.

What shall we name the linelanders?

Students might suggest only boys' names for the linelanders. If so, encourage them to suggest girls' names as well. Perhaps they will think of names that could be either.

Which linelanders can Robin visit?

Only Terry and Shawn.

Can Robin reach Pat?

No. Robin cannot leave the line. The line is the whole universe.

Finite/Infinite, Boundary/No Boundary

The concepts of *finite* and *infinite,* introduced in Lesson 1, are reviewed at the top of the Activity 2c worksheet. They also appear on the optional transparency. These terms apply in all dimensions.

A universe is finite if it has a limited, measurable length/area/volume.

A universe is infinite if it has unlimited length/area/volume.

The concept of a boundary is something different:

A boundary is an edge of space. A traveler who reaches a boundary can go no farther.

As students work in small groups to complete Activity 2c, they may be surprised to realize that the finite/infinite distinction is completely independent of the boundary/no boundary distinction.

When student groups are finished, reconvene to discuss their answers.

Homework

Distribute Homework 2, due tomorrow.

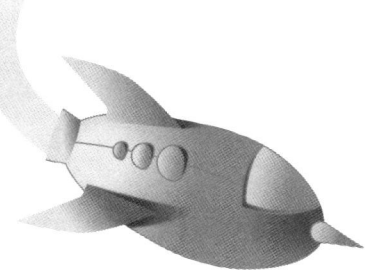

Definitions

1-dimensional   Only one number is required to specify a location; has length but no area.

2-dimensional   Two numbers are required to specify a location; has area but no volume.

3-dimensional   Three numbers are required to specify a location; has volume.

boundary   An edge of space. A traveler who reaches a boundary can go no farther.

finite   Has a limited, measurable length/area/volume.

infinite   Has unlimited length/area/volume.

Activity 2a

Name_____

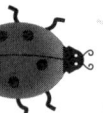

Coordinates

1. Use a globe or world map to locate the major cities whose latitude and longitude are given in the table.

Latitude	Longitude	City
23°30′ S	46°40′ W	São Paulo, Brazil
64°10′ N	21°50′ W	
1°20′ S	36°50′ E	
22°30′ N	88°30′ E	
21°20′ N	157°50′ W	
52°20′ N	4°50′ E	

2. What are the latitude and longitude of your own home town?

Latitude	Longitude	City

3. Hide a small object somewhere in your classroom. Write down the following.

   a. Its distance from the front wall of the classroom.

   b. Its distance from the left wall of the classroom.

   c. Its height above the floor.

   d. A brief description of the object (such as "red pencil").

   After everyone has hidden an object, exchange papers at random and try to find someone else's hidden treasure. If all goes well, the three numbers you wrote down will lead your classmate exactly to your treasure's hiding place. When the game is over, please return your classmate's treasure and clue sheet.

Activity 2a (continued)　　　　　　　　Name

Bonus Problem

Suppose you were at 13° S latitude, 79° W longitude.

a. What major city would be nearest to you?

b. What major city would be farthest away?

Activity 2b   Name_____

Dimensions

1. How would you specify the position of an airplane in Earth's atmosphere? How many numbers are required?

2. How would you specify the position of a sailboat on the ocean? How many numbers are required?

3. How would you specify the position of a train traveling along the rail line from Toronto to Montreal? How many numbers are required?

> Earth's atmosphere is *3-dimensional* because three numbers are required to specify a location.
> The surface of the ocean is *2-dimensional* because two numbers are required to specify a location.
> A line or curve is *1-dimensional* because only one number is required to specify a location.

4. State whether each of the following is 3-dimensional, 2-dimensional, or 1-dimensional by deciding how many numbers are required to specify a point.

    a. Your desktop

    b. A straight line

    c. The circumference of a circle

    d. The inside of a circle

    e. The surface of the moon

    f. The inside of the moon

    g. The surface of a doughnut

Activity 2b (continued)

    h. The surface of your skin

    i. The air inside your classroom

    j. A movie screen

    k. The milk in a milk carton

Bonus Problems

1. How many numbers are required to specify the exact time on a given day? Is time 3-dimensional, 2-dimensional, or 1-dimensional?

2. All colors may be obtained by mixing red, green, and blue light. How many numbers are required to exactly specify a color? Is the set of all colors 3-dimensional, 2-dimensional, or 1-dimensional?

Activity 2c Name_____

Finite/Infinite, Boundary/No Boundary

The concepts of finite and infinite apply in all dimensions.

> A universe is *finite* if it has a limited, measurable length/area/volume.
> A universe is *infinite* if it has unlimited length/area/volume.

The concept of a boundary also applies in all dimensions, but it is different from the concept of finite/infinite.

> A *boundary* is an edge of space. A traveler who reaches a boundary can go no farther.

1. Here are four 1-dimensional universes:

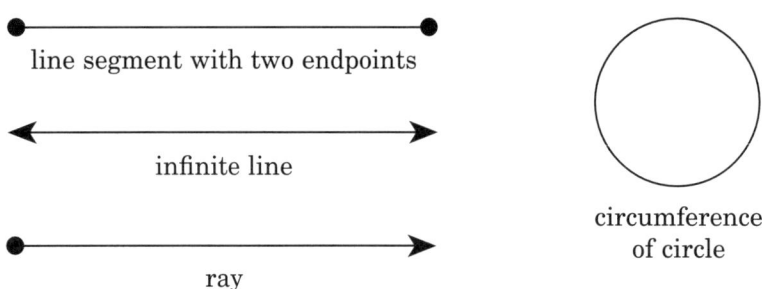

line segment with two endpoints

infinite line

ray

circumference of circle

   a. Estimate the length (or circumference) of each universe in centimeters. If the length is infinite, write "∞ cm."

   b. For each universe that has a boundary, color the boundary points blue.

   c. Draw each universe in its correct place in the table below.

	With boundary	**Without boundary**
Finite		
Infinite		

18 **Wraparound Universe**

Exploring the Shape of Space
©2001 Key Curriculum Press

Activity 2c (continued)   Name_____

2. Here are four 2-dimensional universes:

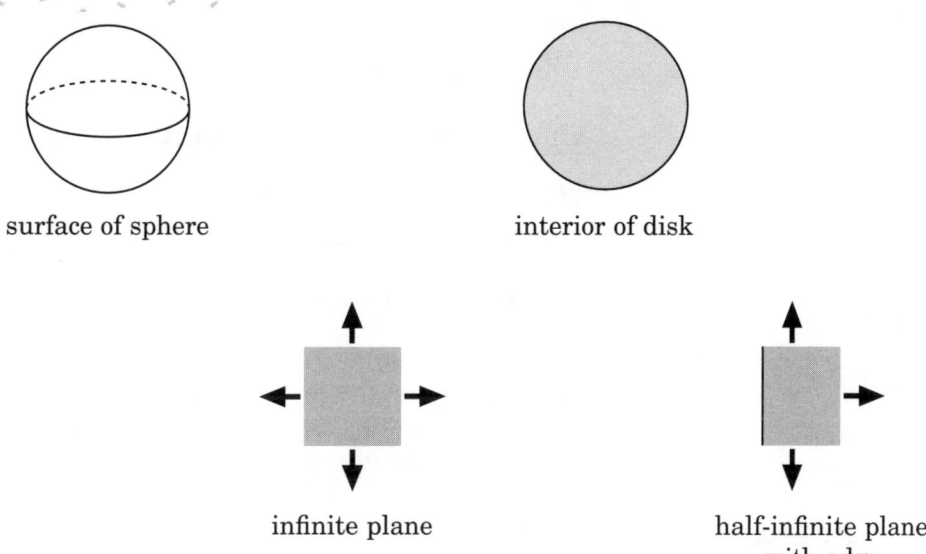

surface of sphere   interior of disk

infinite plane   half-infinite plane with edge

a. Estimate the surface area of each universe in square centimeters. If the area is infinite, write "∞ cm²."

b. For each universe that has a boundary, color the boundary line or curve blue.

c. Draw each universe in its correct place in the table below.

	With boundary	**Without boundary**
Finite		
Infinite		

Bonus Problem

Make a table like the one in Question 2. Invent a 3-dimensional universe for each place in the table. (Don't worry if you find one case much harder than the other three. We'll see examples of it later.)

Exploring the Shape of Space   **Wraparound Universe**

Homework 2

Wraparound Universe

1. Match each word on the left with its definition on the right.

   - finite
   - infinite
   - boundary
   - 1-dimensional
   - 2-dimensional
   - 3-dimensional

   - One number specifies a point.
   - Has a definite, limited length/area/volume.
   - Three numbers specify a point.
   - Has unlimited length/area/volume.
   - Two numbers specify a point.
   - Edge or border.

2. Match each dimension on the left with its description on the right.

   - 1-dimensional
   - 2-dimensional
   - 3-dimensional

   - Has area but no volume.
   - Has volume.
   - Has length but no area.

3. The surface of a sphere is a possible universe for flatlanders.

   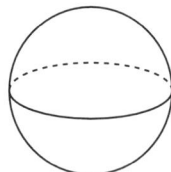

   a. Is the surface 2-dimensional or 3-dimensional? (Hint: How many numbers are required to specify a point on the sphere's surface? Ignore the space inside the sphere.)

   b. Is the surface finite or infinite?

   c. Does the surface have a boundary?

4. Draw a 2-dimensional universe for flatlanders that is infinite and has a boundary.

Homework 2 (continued)   Name_____

Bonus Problem

Draw a linelander.

Where is the linelander's skin?

How many dimensions does the linelander's skin have?

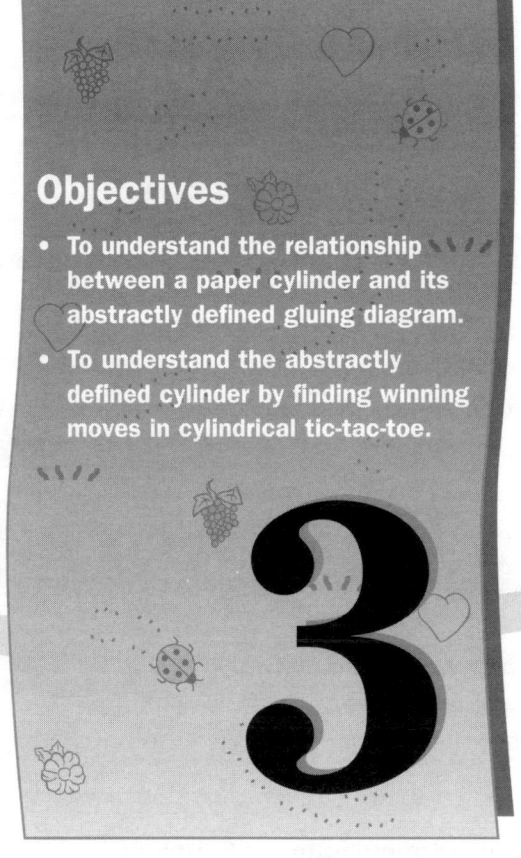

Objectives

- To understand the relationship between a paper cylinder and its abstractly defined gluing diagram.
- To understand the abstractly defined cylinder by finding winning moves in cylindrical tic-tac-toe.

3 Cylindrical Tic-Tac-Toe

Materials

White paper cut into 6 almost-square pieces per sheet (1 or 2 squares per student)

Scissors (1 pair for each student or group)

Tape (several rolls)

Transparency 3: Tic-Tac-Toe (optional)

Activity 3a: Tic-Tac-Toe on a Cylinder

Activity 3b: Equivalent Games

Homework 3: Cylindrical Tic-Tac-Toe

Outline

Location: classroom

10 minutes: Tic-Tac-Toe on Paper Cylinders (whole class and pairs)

10 minutes: Gluing Diagrams (whole class)

10 minutes: Tic-Tac-Toe on a Cylinder (Activity 3a, groups)

20 minutes: Equivalent Games (whole class; Activity 3b, groups)

Vocabulary

cylinder

gluing diagram

equivalent

translation

rotation

reflection

Teacher Notes

Activities

Tic-Tac-Toe on Paper Cylinders

Show students how to set up a cylindrical tic-tac-toe board. For each game, draw a 3-by-3 tic-tac-toe board on a small paper square, and tape it to make a **cylinder**.

Have students choose partners to play several games of tic-tac-toe on a cylinder using the small paper squares.

After the students have played several games, draw the first tic-tac-toe board shown at left on a full-size piece of paper.

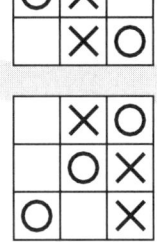

For the cylindrical tic-tac-toe game I drew, has any player already won?

Ask a volunteer to tape the square to make a cylinder, and ask another volunteer to cut it open to show the three-in-a-row more clearly (as shown in the second game at left).

Gluing Diagrams

Is the cylindrical tic-tac-toe board 2-dimensional or 3-dimensional?

It's 2-dimensional, because two numbers specify a point.

The cylinder is a universe for 2-dimensional flatlanders, even though we constructed it in 3-dimensional space. Bending a surface in space is no problem for us, but when we study 3-dimensional universes later in the unit, we don't want to have to bend them in 4-dimensional space! It is possible to visualize 4-dimensional space, but it won't be necessary. Instead, let's play cylindrical tic-tac-toe using only two dimensions for our drawing. That way, when we get to 3-dimensional universes later on, we'll know how to draw them using only three dimensions for our drawings.

(Note: Students interested in 4-dimensional space may be directed to Edwin Abbott's classic, *Flatland*. In our 3-dimensional world, time is a fourth dimension, but Abbott's book presents a fourth spatial dimension, in which case time becomes a fifth dimension.)

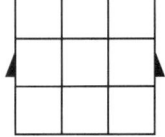

Draw a tic-tac-toe board on the chalkboard, marking the left and right sides with arrows to indicate that those edges are (abstractly) glued together to make a **gluing diagram** of a cylinder. (Alternatively, show the first figure on Transparency 3.)

Draw two **X**s as shown at left.

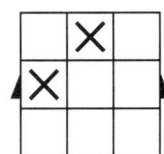

24   Cylindrical Tic-Tac-Toe

Teacher Notes

Where does X move to win?

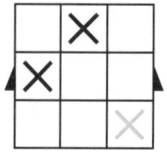

Let the students play a couple of games of cylindrical tic-tac-toe on this board as a class. Divide the class into two teams. Have each team send a representative to the board to mark the team's moves. The representative does not select the move but merely records the team's consensus.

Tic-Tac-Toe on a Cylinder

Have students complete Activity 3a. As they work, circulate around the room monitoring their progress, asking questions, and helping with any questions the students raise.

Equivalent Games

Draw the diagrams below on the chalkboard (or display Transparency 3). When most of the students have finished Activity 3a, redirect the class's attention to the chalkboard.

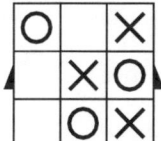 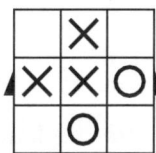 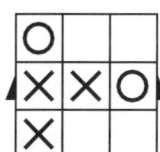 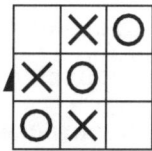

Two games are considered *equivalent* if they yield the same game on a cylinder. Which of these cylindrical tic-tac-toe games are equivalent?

Abstract approach. *For each column in one game, see whether there is an identical column in any of the other games. As it turns out, the first game has the same columns as the fourth game, so they will be identical when rolled into a cylinder. Similarly, the second and third games have the same columns, although one is upside down relative to the other.*

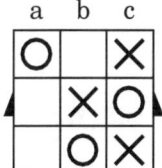 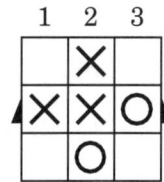 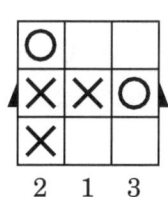 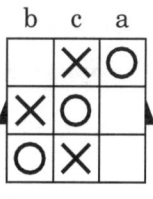

Concrete approach. *If the students are in doubt, ask volunteers to draw the games onto sheets of paper and tape them into cylinders. The students will see that the first and last games yield the same game on a cylinder and are therefore equivalent. The two middle games are also equivalent, even though the cylinder for one must be turned upside down to match the other.*

Teacher Notes

Have students complete Activity 3b while you circulate about the room asking and answering questions.

Especially in the younger middle school grades, it's not so important that students be able to find all equivalent games systematically. Eager students, however, may want to do so. Many middle school students happily find equivalent games, using ***translations, reflections,*** and ***rotations*** in a purely informal and intuitive way. With older students, you might want to develop the translations, reflections, and rotations more systematically by writing the terms on the board and discussing examples. For example, in Question 2 on the activity sheet, you may ask students to label each equivalent game as one of the following:

- equivalent by *translation*
- equivalent by *horizontal reflection* (possibly followed by a translation)
- equivalent by *vertical reflection* (possibly followed by a translation)
- equivalent by *rotation* (possibly followed by a translation)

The purpose of this exercise is to get students thinking about equivalent games, with the ultimate goal that, when they see a gluing diagram, they understand that it represents a cylinder and that the precise location of the cut is unimportant. There are many approaches, and students should be encouraged to develop their own ideas. If they get stuck, here are some simple approaches to Question 2:

- *Approach 1.* **Label the columns of the original game a, b, and c. How can these labels be rearranged in the equivalent games? There are 3! equals 6 ways to arrange them across the top, namely, abc, acb, bac, bca, cab, and cba, and the same 6 ways to arrange them across the bottom. This gives all 2 times 6 equals 12 possibilities.**

- *Approach 2.* **The three Os form an L shape.**

  Consider the O in the central square of the original game. Which squares could it go to?

  Any of the three squares in the middle row.

  Once the central O has found a home, which squares could the O below it go to?

  It must go to a square above or below the central O's new home.

26   Cylindrical Tic-Tac-Toe   *Exploring the Shape of Space*

Once those first two Os have found their homes, which squares could the remaining O go to?

It must go to a square to the left or right of the second O's new home.

This gives all 3 times 2 times 2 equals 12 possibilities.

- *Approach 3.* **Older students familiar with translations and reflections may classify the equivalent games as shown in the answer key.**

Homework

Distribute Homework 3, due tomorrow.

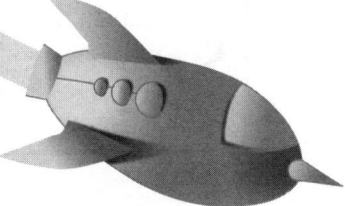

Transparency 3

Tic-Tac-Toe

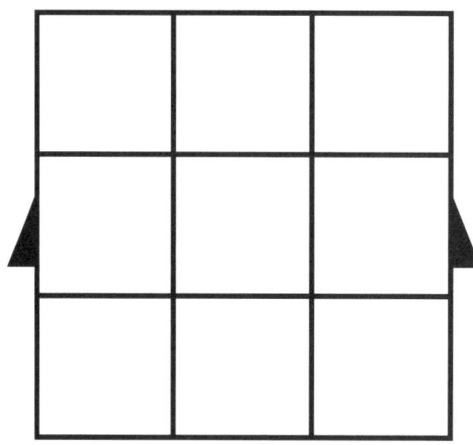

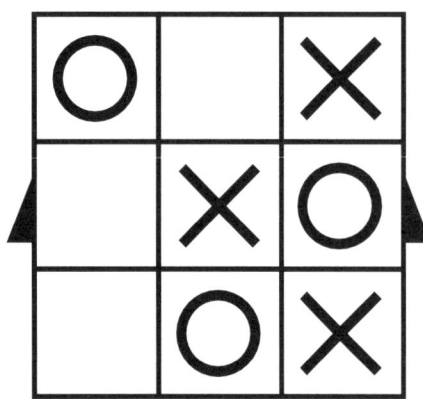
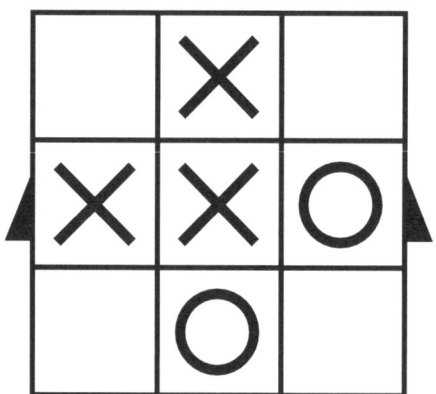

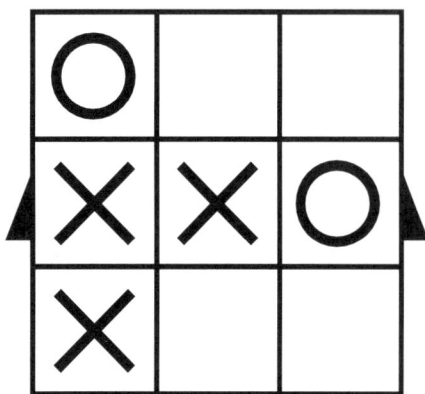
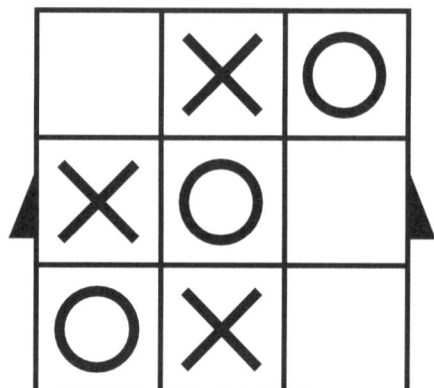

28 **Cylindrical Tic-Tac-Toe**

Exploring the Shape of Space
©2001 Key Curriculum Press

Activity 3a   Name_____

Tic-Tac-Toe on a Cylinder

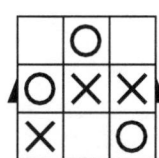   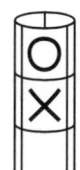

The small arrows on the gluing
diagram mean the left and
right sides get glued . . .   . . . to form a cylinder.

1. In each of the following cylindrical tic-tac-toe games, decide whether one of the players has already won. If so, draw a line through the three-in-a-row.

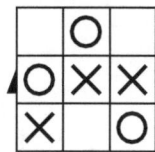 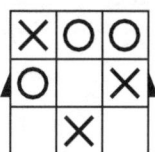 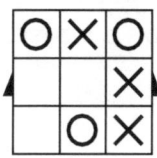 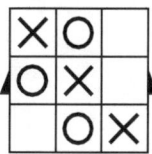

2. Play a few games of cylindrical tic-tac-toe with a friend.

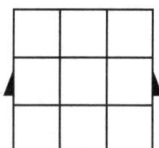 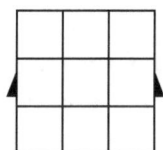 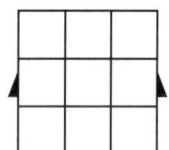 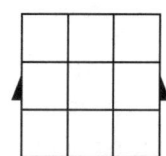

3. In each of the following cylindrical tic-tac-toe games, mark X's best move. If X wins on this move, draw a line through the three-in-a-row.

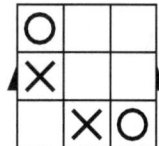 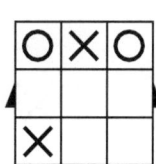 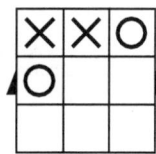 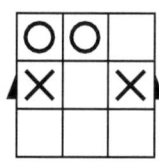

Exploring the Shape of Space **Cylindrical Tic-Tac-Toe** **29**
©2001 Key Curriculum Press

Activity 3b　　　　　　　　　　　　Name_____

Equivalent Games

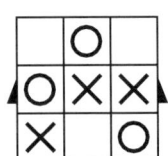 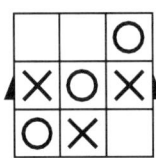　　　　　　　

Even though these two games look different, . . .　　　　. . . they give identical games on a cylinder.

There are two ways to verify that the games above are equivalent.

Method 1. Cut a sheet of plain paper into six small squares. Copy each game onto a small square, roll it into a cylinder, and tape it. The two games shown above become identical on cylinders.

Method 2. Label the columns of one game and check whether the other game contains the same columns, but in a different order.

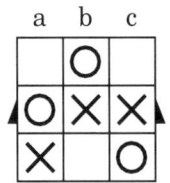 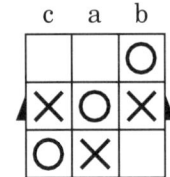

1. Which of the following cylindrical tic-tac-toe games are equivalent? In other words, if you taped each square's left and right sides together, which ones would give you the same game on a cylinder? You may use either method described above or a method of your own. Each game is equivalent to at least one other game.

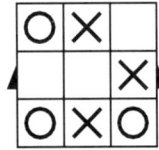 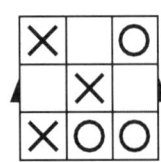 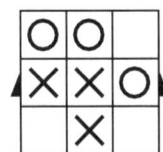 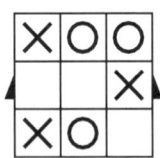

2. On the back of this page, draw all cylindrical tic-tac-toe games equivalent to the one below.

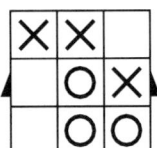

30　　Cylindrical Tic-Tac-Toe

Homework 3

Cylindrical Tic-Tac-Toe

1. Mark X's winning move in each of the following cylindrical tic-tac-toe games, and draw a line through the three-in-a-row.

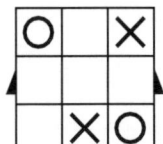 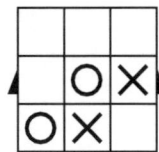 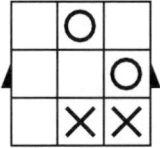 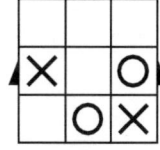

2. Which of the following cylindrical tic-tac-toe games are equivalent? There are more than two!

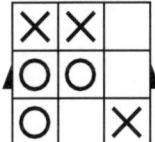 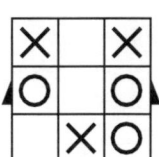 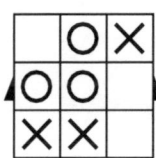 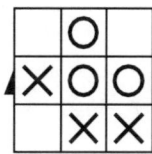

You may choose from (at least) two approaches to this problem. The first approach is to draw the games on pieces of paper, tape them into cylinders, and see which games are the same. The second approach is to label the columns of one game and look for matching columns in the other games.

Bonus Problem

In traditional tic-tac-toe, two good players will always play to a draw. Is that also true in cylindrical tic-tac-toe? On the back of this page explain why or why not.

Super Bonus Problem

In cylindrical tic-tac-toe, can two players cooperate to play to a draw? On the back of this page, give an example of a game that ends in a draw or explain why this can't happen.

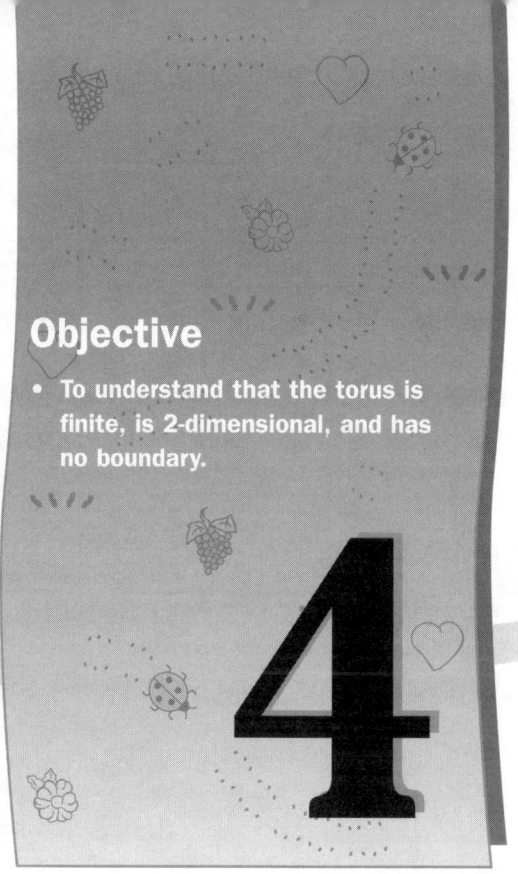

Objective

- To understand that the torus is finite, is 2-dimensional, and has no boundary.

Torus Games

Materials

Computers with Java-capable Web browsers (one for every two students)

Computer projection system (optional)

Torus Games Web pages (on CD-ROM and available online)

Transparency 4: Torus Introduction (optional)

Homework 4: Torus Games

Outline

Location: computer lab

5 minutes: Introduction to the Torus (whole class)

30+ minutes: Torus Games (pairs or small groups)

Vocabulary

torus

Teacher Notes

Activities

Introduction to the Torus

This quick introduction presents the torus and the game software. It is best to work together as a class, either using a projection system if your computer lab has one, or gathering the students around a single monitor if they can all see it clearly. If this is not possible, you can display Transparency 4 as you discuss the behavior of objects in the torus.

Begin on the main page (**TorusGames/index.html**).

Yesterday we played tic-tac-toe on a cylinder. Today we are going to use the computers to play several games on a new surface.

Click to the Introduction. Grab the heart with the mouse.

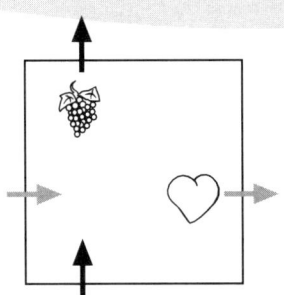

What do you think will happen when I drag the heart past the right edge of the square?

It comes back at the left.

What will happen when I drag the grapes past the top of the square?

They come back at the bottom.

This space is called a torus. It's like a cylinder both horizontally and vertically.

You can illustrate this comment by bending a sheet of paper to form first a vertical cylinder, then a horizontal cylinder, as you speak.

You can scroll the whole board by dragging with the right mouse button (Windows) or with the Command key held down (Macintosh).

Scroll the whole board.

How many dimensions does the torus have?

It's 2-dimensional. Two numbers specify a point.

Is the torus finite or infinite?

It's finite. It has a limited, measurable area, and it contains only four objects: the heart, the grapes, the flower, and the ladybug. (For clarity the flower and ladybug are suppressed from the above figure and Transparency 4.)

What's its approximate area, in square centimeters?

Answers will vary depending on the projection method. On an ordinary computer monitor the game might be only 10 cm by 10 cm, with an area of 100 cm^2. With a projection system, the game could be as large as 1 m by 1 m, with an area of 1 m^2 or 10,000 cm^2.

34   Torus Games   Exploring the Shape of Space

Teacher Notes

Does it have a boundary?

No. Flatlanders living in it could travel in any direction they wanted and never hit an edge.

That's right. A *torus* is a 2-dimensional finite shape that has no boundary. It is different from a cylinder because a cylinder does have a boundary.

Return to the main page, and click to tic-tac-toe. With the whole class, play one quick game against the computer. When appropriate, ask students why the computer is making the moves it is (for example, to block a spot where the class might win). Show students how to use the game's menu to switch from **human vs. computer** to **human vs. human** mode.

Torus Games

Have students choose partners and play the games.

You may play the six games—tic-tac-toe, maze, crossword, word search, jigsaw puzzle, and chess—in any order. Please play each of the first five games at least once so you'll be prepared for the homework. Try the torus chess, too, if you know how to play regular chess.

For educational as well as social reasons, it's best for the students to work in pairs or small groups. For the tic-tac-toe and chess games, encourage them to try **human vs. human** as well as **human vs. computer** mode. However, tell them not to switch from **torus** mode to **Klein bottle** mode—the Klein bottle is saved for Lesson 8.

As the students play the games, circulate about the room answering their questions and congratulating them for their successes. If they get stuck, ask questions to get them thinking without giving away the answers. For example, if students are stuck in a maze, suggest they try working backward from the cheese to the mouse. Scrolling the board also helps.

Homework

Distribute Homework 4, due tomorrow.

Students May Wonder, Where's the Doughnut?

The torus explored in this lesson, the square with opposite sides glued, is a flat torus. This lesson intentionally omits the doughnut-surface realization of a torus in favor of the flat torus, for two reasons:

- The flat torus leads easily to the 3-dimensional torus universe in Lesson 6.

Exploring the Shape of Space

Teacher Notes

- Astronomical observations suggest that the real universe, if it is a torus, is a flat torus.

The doughnut surface and the flat torus are topologically equivalent (see Homework 5, Question 4), but the doughnut surface has varying curvature, while the flat torus has constant zero curvature like the ordinary Euclidean plane. Students will see the doughnut surface when they view the video in Lesson 6.

Torus Introduction

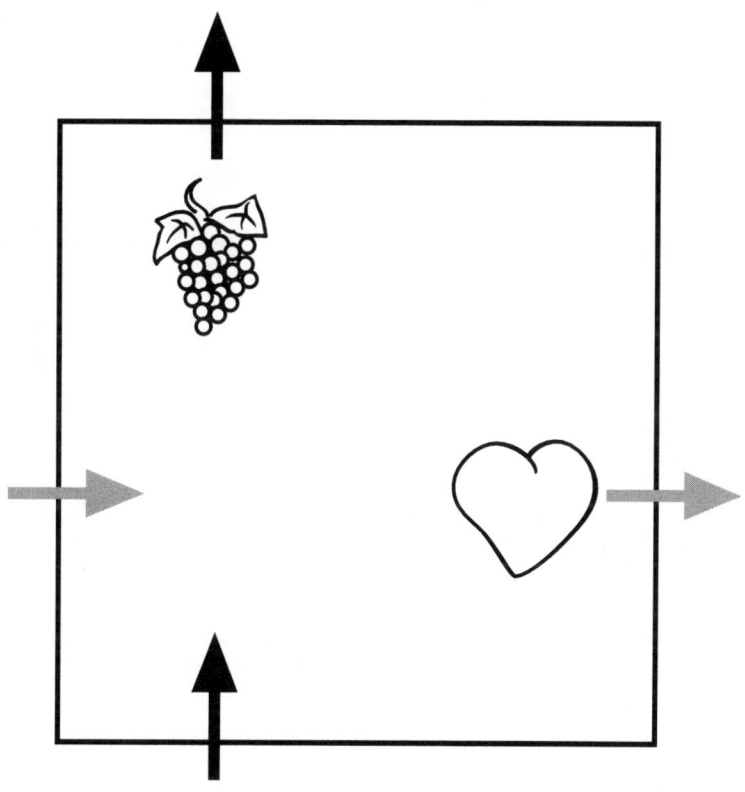

Homework 4

Torus Games

1. Draw a path leading the mouse to the cheese in the torus maze at right.

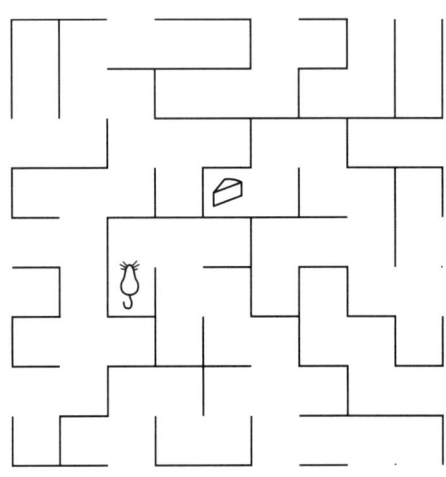

2. Circle the word *torus* in the torus word search puzzle at right.

c	r	u	z	s	m
p	a	h	s	a	e
o	t	o	p	i	e
l	s	a	a	l	t
o	t	i	c	o	u
x	r	a	e	r	r

3. a. Is a torus finite or infinite?

   b. Does a torus have a boundary?

   c. Is a torus 2-dimensional or 3-dimensional?

Homework 4 (continued)  Name_____

4. a. Use this sheet of paper to represent a torus. The ladybug crawling northeast across the top of the page will return at the bottom of the page. To see how, roll the page into a cylinder (so the top and bottom edges meet), and extend the ladybug's path forward a few centimeters. Now unroll the cylinder and look at where the ladybug's path enters the bottom of the page. What direction is she heading?

b. The ladybug in the torus at right walks in a straight line until she returns to her starting point. Draw her path.

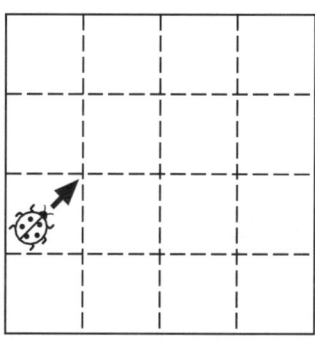

Bonus Problems

1. Draw the path of a ladybug who walks in a straight line until she returns to her starting point if she always walks as follows.

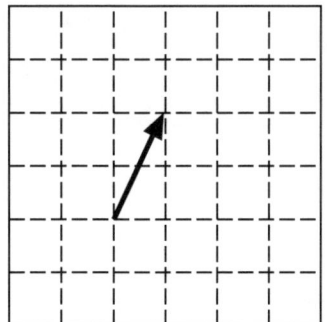

a. 2 units northward for every 1 unit eastward

b. 3 units northward for every 2 units eastward

2. Make your own maze, crossword puzzle, or word search puzzle on a torus, and challenge a classmate to solve it. You can design your puzzle with pencil and paper, or, if you have access to a computer, you can play the Torus Games online at **http://www.keypress.com/space/** and use the built-in Crossword Puzzle Editor or Word Search Editor.

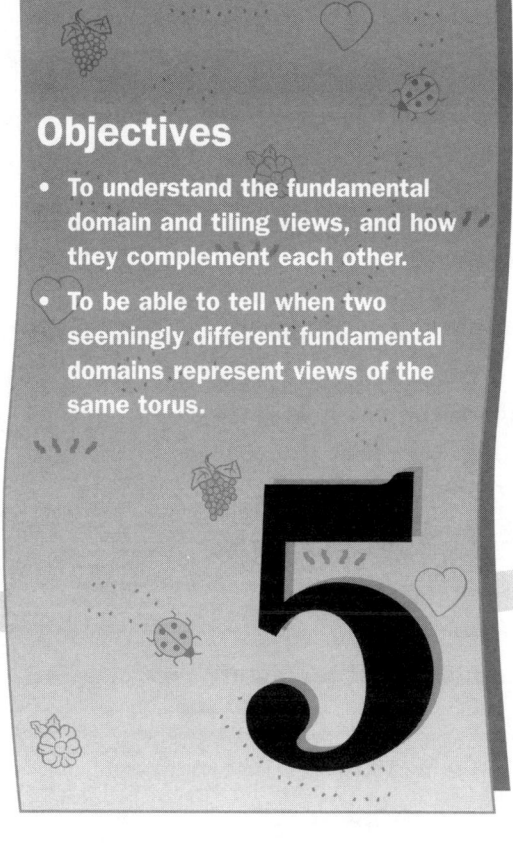

Objectives

- To understand the fundamental domain and tiling views, and how they complement each other.
- To be able to tell when two seemingly different fundamental domains represent views of the same torus.

5 More Torus Games

Materials

Computers with Java-capable Web browsers

Computer projection system (optional)

Torus Games Web pages (on CD-ROM and available online)

Transparency 5: Tiling View Introduction (optional)

Activity 5: Games on a Torus

Homework 5: More Torus Games

Outline

Location: computer lab

5 minutes: Tiling View and Fundamental Domain (whole class)

30+ minutes: Games on a Torus (Activity 5; pairs or groups)

Vocabulary

fundamental domain

tiling view

Teacher Notes

Activities

Tiling View and Fundamental Domain

Ask students to direct their attention to the projection system (if you have one), gather around your monitor (if they all fit), or otherwise just follow along using their own computers as you show Transparency 5.

From the main page (**TorusGames/index.html**), click to the Introduction. Grab the ladybug and move it to the center of the square (or show the first figure on the transparency).

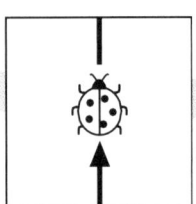

What does the ladybug see when she looks forward?

Her line of sight wraps around the torus and she sees her own backside (second figure on the transparency).

That's right. The ladybug has the illusion of seeing another copy of herself, one unit ahead.

Point to where that image would appear to be (third figure).

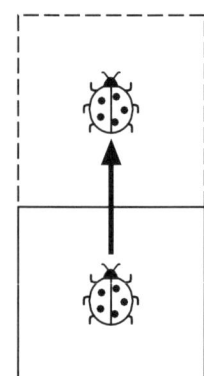

What does the ladybug see when she looks to the right?

Her line of sight wraps around, and she has the illusion of seeing another copy of herself, one unit to the right (fourth figure).

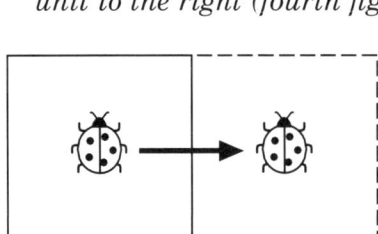

What does the ladybug see along a 45° line?

Another image of herself (fifth figure).

You can have the computer draw the repeating images the ladybug sees.

Use the menu to switch from **fundamental domain** view to **tiling** view (last figure).

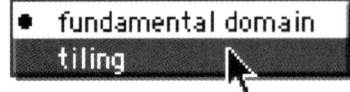

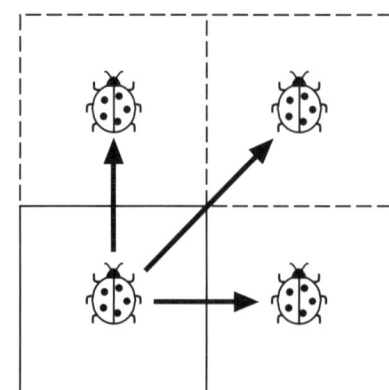

42   **More Torus Games** *Exploring the Shape of Space*

What will happen when we move the heart?

All its images move simultaneously.

The ladybug has the illusion of seeing an infinite universe, as we see in the tiling view, but really there is only one heart, as we see when we look at the fundamental domain. The ladybug sees many images of the heart because her line of sight can reach it in many different directions.

Is it possible to see more than one heart if we look only in the fundamental domain?

No. Everything in the fundamental domain appears once.

The fundamental domain and tiling views are complementary views of the torus:

- The fundamental domain view shows correctly that the torus is finite, but incorrectly suggests that it has a boundary.
- The tiling view shows correctly that the torus has no boundary, but incorrectly suggests that it's infinite.

To understand the torus fully, try to keep both views in your head at once so you can see that the torus is finite yet has no boundary.

(Note: The crossword puzzle, jigsaw puzzle, and chess game offer the tiling view, but the tic-tac-toe, maze, and word search do not, because the tiling view makes those games too easy.)

Games on a Torus

Distribute Activity 5 and circulate around the room as the students work on it, monitoring their progress and asking helpful questions as necessary. When students finish the activity sheet, they may play freely with the games until the end of the period.

Homework

Distribute Homework 5, due tomorrow.

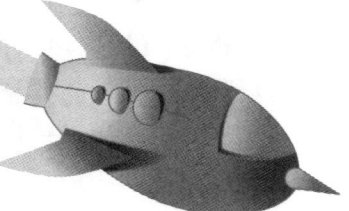

Transparency 5

Tiling View Introduction

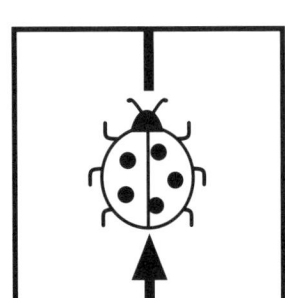
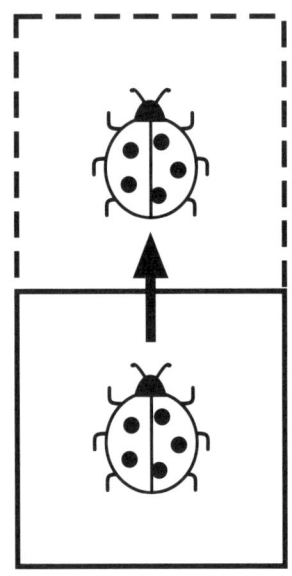
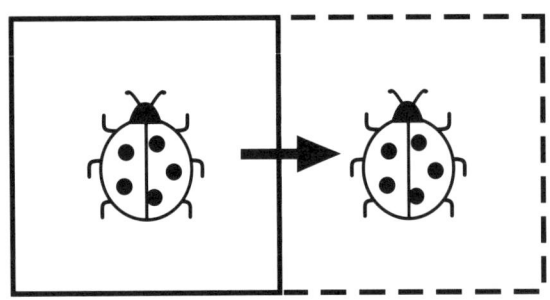
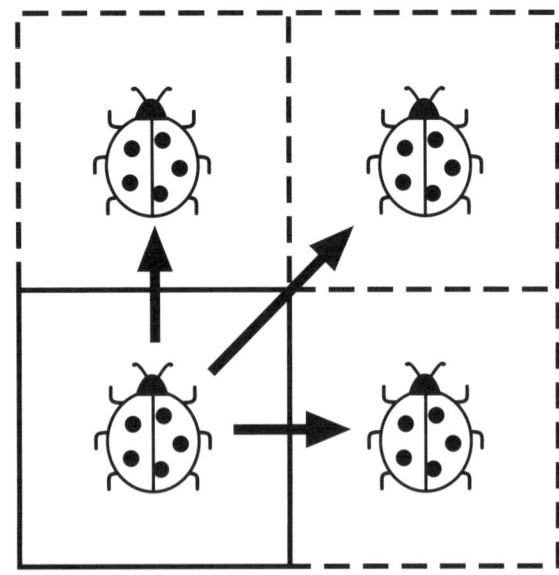

- fundamental domain
- tiling

44 **More Torus Games**

Exploring the Shape of Space
©2001 Key Curriculum Press

Activity 5

Name_____

Games on a Torus

1. Open the first torus crossword puzzle, and type in the two words shown at right. Switch from the **fundamental domain** view to the **tiling** view, and sketch what you see.

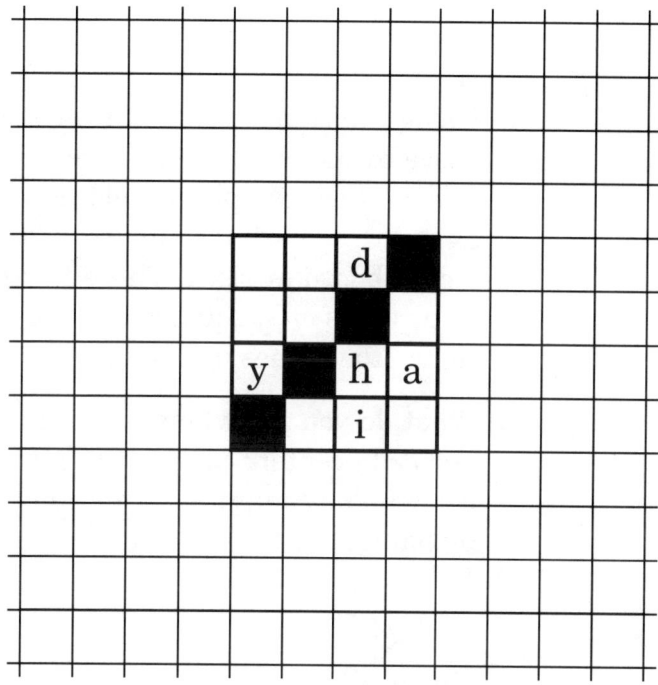

2. Extend the drawing of the tic-tac-toe game shown at right from **fundamental domain** view to **tiling** view. (The tic-tac-toe computer game doesn't offer **tiling** view, so do this by hand.)

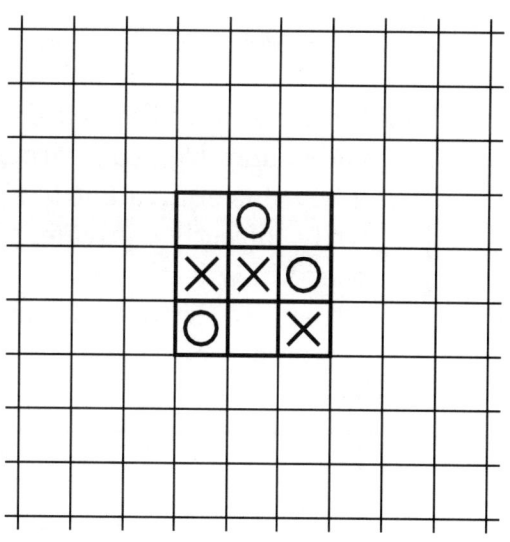

3. Assemble the first torus jigsaw puzzle—the one with the colored flowers.

   a. Imagine that our ladybug friend begins at the red flower and climbs up the vine. Which other flowers does she pass on that same vine? (Hint: It may be helpful to scroll the picture as you trace along the vine.)

   b. How many different vines are there?

Exploring the Shape of Space
©2001 Key Curriculum Press

More Torus Games   45

Activity 5 (continued)   Name _____

4. Open the torus tic-tac-toe computer game, switch to **human vs. human** mode, and set up the board shown at right.

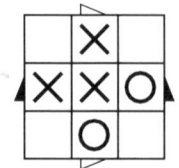

   a. Using the right mouse button, drag the board one space to the left and one space up. (If you are using a Macintosh computer, hold down the Command key as you drag with the mouse.) Sketch the result in the empty board at right. These two pictures look different as pictures on a square, but they are equivalent as tic-tac-toe games on a torus.

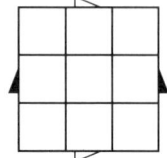

   b. What do you get when you rotate the board 180 degrees about its center? Sketch the result in the empty board below. (The computer game can't do this—you must do it by hand.)

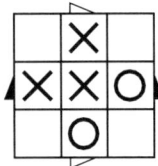   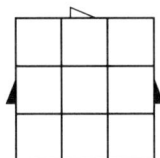

5. Set up each of the boards below in the tic-tac-toe computer game, and drag each around with the right mouse button. If a board is equivalent to the first board in Question 4b, write "directly equivalent." If it's equivalent to the second board in Question 4b, write "equivalent by rotation." Otherwise, write "not equivalent."

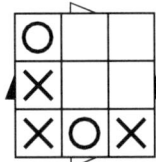   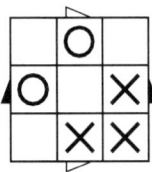   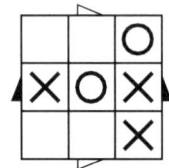

Activity 5 (continued)

Bonus Problems

1. Does the first move matter in torus tic-tac-toe? In other words, are all first moves equivalent? Explain.

2. If the first player in torus tic-tac-toe takes the upper left corner, how many nonequivalent moves does the second player have to choose from?

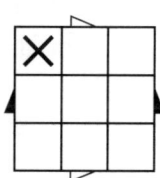

Homework 5   Name_____

More Torus Games

1. Which of the following torus tic-tac-toe games are equivalent? There are more than two! Remember, in a torus you may scroll the pieces up and down as well as right and left. Rotations and reflections are okay too!

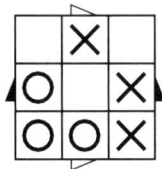 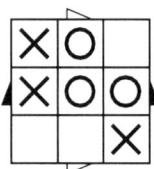 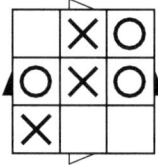 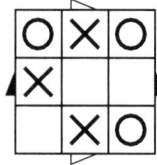 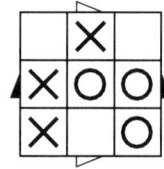

2. On this tiling view of a torus picture, mark a fundamental domain.

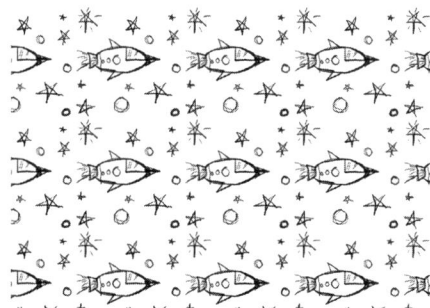

3. Make a drawing on a torus. You may use any subject and any medium (such as colored pencils, paints, or crayons). Be creative and make use of the torus's wraparound nature. Use the grid at right, which shows a central fundamental domain and its eight neighbors. You may want to experiment on scrap paper before making your final drawing in the space at right. After you have decided on a design, draw it in the central square (the fundamental domain) and then copy it into the other squares to make a tiling view.

4. If you physically glue a square's left and right edges, you get a cylinder. If you then try to glue the top to the bottom, and the square is made of paper, you get a crumpled mess. But if the square were made of easily stretchable rubber, what shape would you get when you glued the top of the cylinder to the bottom?

Bonus Problems

1. Which of the following torus mazes are equivalent?

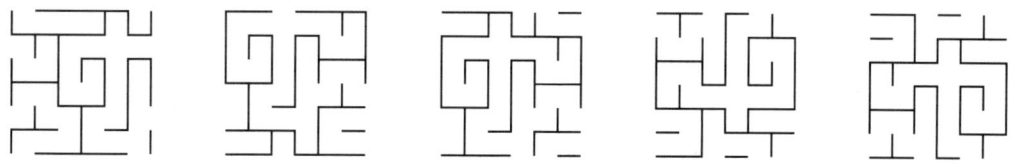

2. For chess players: Show how black can checkmate white in one move in the torus chess game shown below.

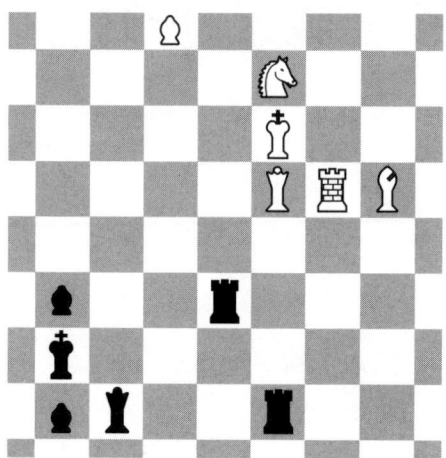

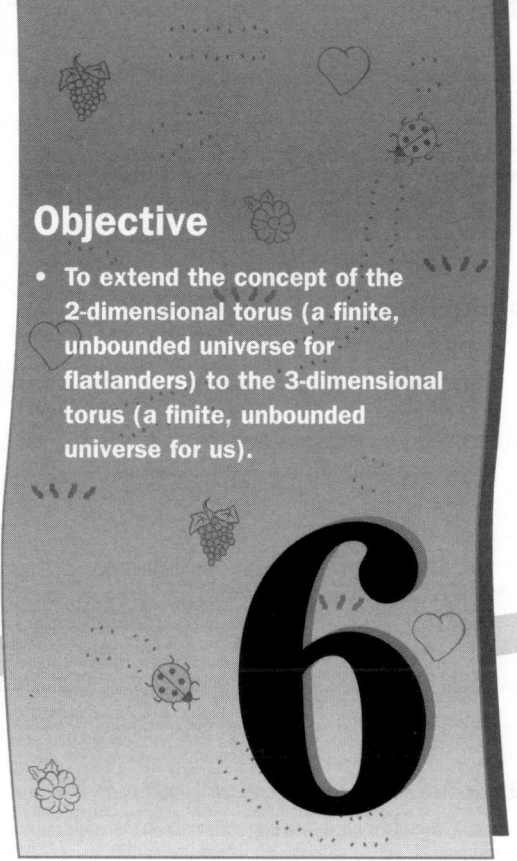

The 3-Torus

Objective
- To extend the concept of the 2-dimensional torus (a finite, unbounded universe for flatlanders) to the 3-dimensional torus (a finite, unbounded universe for us).

Materials

The Shape of Space video and VCR

Video Guide 1: *The Shape of Space,* Part 1

Transparency 6: The Real Universe (replaces Activity 6a)

Activity 6a: The Real Universe

Activity 6b: Torus Dimensions

Homework 6: The 3-Torus

Reading: Cosmology

Celestial Map: Locating the Andromeda Galaxy (optional)

Outline

Location: classroom

5 minutes: Introduction to the 3-Torus (whole class)

15 minutes: The Shape of Space video (first half)

10 minutes: The Real Universe (Activity 6a; groups)

20 minutes: Torus Dimensions (Activity 6b; groups)

Vocabulary

2-torus

3-torus

Teacher Notes

Activities

Introduction to the 3-Torus

Was the torus in yesterday's computer games a 2-dimensional universe or a 3-dimensional universe?

Two-dimensional.

How can we apply the idea of the torus to make a 3-dimensional universe?

Give students some time to think and to explore their ideas. Don't be discouraged if they don't make much progress—this is a hard question! If they don't solve the problem on their own, ask this question:

What geometrical shape is like a square, only 3-dimensional?

A cube.

So, instead of starting with a 2-dimensional square, let's start with a 3-dimensional block of space. Imagine the rectangular block of space defined by the classroom.

Walk to the front of the classroom and point to the wall (or chalkboard).

If I go out the front wall, where will I come back?

The back wall.

Walk over to a side wall of the classroom.

If I go out this wall, where will I come back?

The opposite wall.

If I fly up through the ceiling, where will I come back?

The floor.

This space is called a 3-dimensional torus, or *3-torus* for short. The torus on which you were playing the computer games yesterday is called a 2-dimensional torus, or *2-torus* for short.

It's always a good idea to write the new vocabulary words on the board.

When you look forward in the 3-torus, what do you see?

The class sees another image of itself, viewed from behind.

What do you see looking to the side?

Another image of the class.

When you look up?

The bottoms of our feet.

Teacher Notes

The Shape of Space Video (first half)

Read, display, or give students copies of the video guide questions. Show the first half of the video *The Shape of Space,* stopping at the end of the flight in the 3-torus, at the point where the narrator says "This isn't the only possible shape for space." (If you are omitting Lessons 7 through 9, you may show the whole animation at this point.) Discuss the answers to the questions in the video guide, as well as any other questions or comments the students may have.

The Real Universe

Display Transparency 6 or give students copies of Activity 6a. Have students break into small groups to discuss the questions and write answers. When they are done, reconvene the class to compare the different groups' ideas.

After students have discussed their ideas, mention that real experiments are under way to test whether space is a 3-torus:

Scientists have recently found a way to test whether space is a 3-torus. In the years 2001 to 2003, a small NASA satellite will measure the radiation remaining from the Big Bang; beginning in about 2007, a European Space Agency satellite will make even more precise measurements. If the universe is small enough that we can see the same region of space in two different directions in the sky, then the radiation arriving from those two directions will have approximately the same temperature pattern. Such an observation may tell us whether the real universe is a 3-torus or whether it has some other shape.

Torus Dimensions

Have students return to their small groups to complete Activity 6b. The activity will help students gain a deeper understanding of what a 3-torus universe would be like.

Homework

Distribute Homework 6, due tomorrow. To make a deeper connection between the 3-torus and the real universe, distribute the reading on cosmology and the star chart for locating the Andromeda galaxy, and ask students to answer the reading comprehension questions.

Further Study

Students may do research projects on connections to the real world, beginning either from the reading and the references cited there or from the Web. Some sample topics for students' projects are listed on the following page.

Exploring the Shape of Space

Teacher Notes

- *Sample Topic 1.* How have different cultures explained the universe and its origins? Students could investigate a specific culture in depth, such as the ancient Chinese, the Babylonians, the Arabs in the Middle Ages, or a Native American culture; or they could compare different cultures.
- *Sample Topic 2.* How did the Europeans' view of the universe evolve over the millennia, and what caused the changes?
- *Sample Topic 3.* What are the goals and methods of current research on the origin of the universe? Students might begin by searching the Web for "Microwave Anisotropy Probe" or checking for leads at **http://www.keypress.com/space/**.

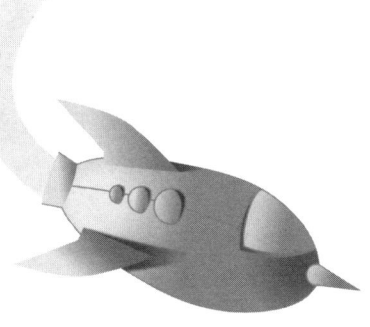

Video Guide 1

The Shape of Space, Part 1

1. What does the video suggest as three possible shapes for the flatlanders' universe?

2. How is the doughnut surface represented in only two dimensions?

3. Why does the video represent the flatlanders' universe in only two dimensions? Why not use the original 3-dimensional pictures?

4. Explain how the flatlanders can see the back of their own spaceship.

5. Explain how the 3-dimensional humans can see the back of their own spaceship.

6. Is the humans' 3-torus universe finite or infinite? Does it have a boundary?

The Real Universe

1. Do you think the real universe could be a 3-torus?

2. What experiments could we do to find out?

3. What are some of the practical difficulties with these experiments?

Activity 6a

The Real Universe

1. Do you think the real universe could be a 3-torus?

2. What experiments could we do to find out?

3. What are some of the practical difficulties with these experiments?

Activity 6b

Torus Dimensions

1. Some flatlanders live in a 2-torus that is 3 light-years wide and 6 light-years long.

   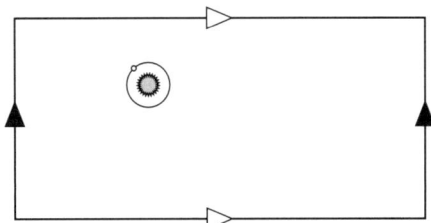

   a. Sketch the tiling view of their universe.

   b. In what direction(s) do they see the nearest image(s) of their solar system?

   c. How far away are the nearest images?

   d. Draw a dotted line (in the original fundamental domain, not the tiling view) showing the path the light takes to reach them.

Activity 6b (continued)   Name_____

e. On the seventeenth day of Csir in the year 3509, some flatlanders look through a telescope at one of the nearest images. Do they see their solar system as it is on Csir 17, 3509, or as it was on some other date? If they see it as it was on some other date, state when and explain why.

2. Suppose the real universe is a 3-torus made from a rectangular fundamental domain 150 million light-years wide, 200 million light-years high, and 250 million light-years long.

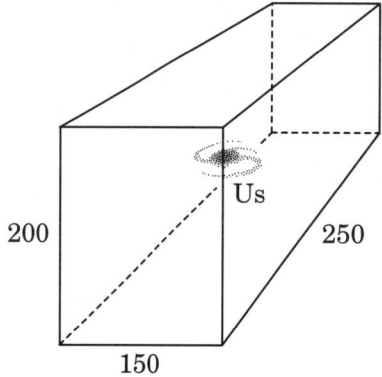

a. In what direction(s) would we humans see the nearest images of ourselves?

b. How far away are our nearest images?

c. Draw a dotted line in the fundamental domain above showing the path the light takes to reach us.

d. On June 17, 2017, some humans use the Hubble Space Telescope to take a picture of the nearest image of our Milky Way galaxy. Do they see the Milky Way as it is on June 17, 2017? If they see it as it was at some other time, state when and explain why.

Activity 6b (continued)   Name_____

Bonus Problem

Have you ever been in a barbershop or another room with mirrors on two opposite walls? What did you see?

How is the image you see in the mirrored room similar to the image you would see in a 3-torus of similar size? How is it different?

Homework 6

The 3-Torus

1. a. Is the 3-torus finite or infinite?

   b. Does the 3-torus have a boundary?

   c. Is the 3-torus 2-dimensional or 3-dimensional?

2. Each 2-torus below has a familiar shape shaded on it. Give the name of each shape. (Hint: Try drawing a tiling view.)

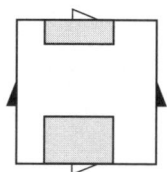 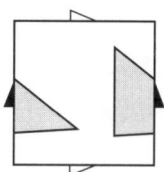 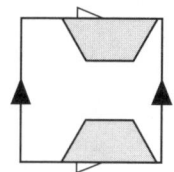 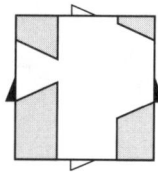

3. Each 3-torus below has a familiar solid drawn in it. Give the name of each solid.

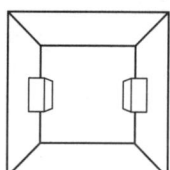 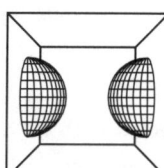 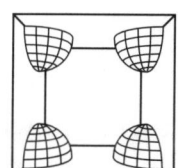 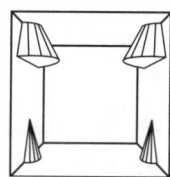

4. Suppose a 3-torus is made from a rectangular block of space 500 meters by 300 meters by 400 meters. What is the shortest distance you can travel (in a straight line) to return to your starting point?

Homework 6 (continued)

Bonus Problem

The inhabitants of a 3-torus universe want to construct two space stations. For efficiency, they want to position the space stations as far away from each other as possible. Make a sketch showing where to place them.

Super Bonus Problem

If you know the Pythagorean theorem, you can use it to solve this problem. Suppose the 3-torus universe in the preceding Bonus Problem is made from a rectangular block of space 600 kilometers by 800 kilometers by 2400 kilometers. How far apart will the two space stations be?

Cosmology

The ancient Greek philosophers had different ideas about space. Some, led by Leucippus (ca. 480–ca. 420 B.C.) and his student Democritus (ca. 460–ca. 370 B.C.), believed the universe to be infinite. Others, led by Aristotle (384–322 B.C.) and his followers, thought space was a finite ball, with Earth at its center and a spherical boundary. Aristotle's view prevailed, and his concept of a finite universe went largely unquestioned for 2000 years, until the late sixteenth century.

In the sixteenth century, philosophers took a more scientific approach to the study of nature. In particular, astronomers discovered that different stars lay at different distances from Earth, all well beyond the boundary that Aristotle imagined. Philosophers rejected Aristotle's concept of the universe and instead imagined an infinite universe. Still, the change in thinking did not come easily: Giordano Bruno (1548–1600) was burned at the stake, apparently because his belief in an infinite universe with infinitely many inhabited worlds challenged authority.

In the mid-nineteenth century, Georg Riemann (1826–1866) found a way to avoid the idea of an infinite universe without returning to Aristotle's idea of a boundary. He proposed the hypersphere as a model for space. The *hypersphere* is the surface of a 4-dimensional ball, just as an ordinary sphere is the surface of a 3-dimensional ball. Like an ordinary sphere, the hypersphere is finite and has no troublesome boundary. But the surface of an ordinary sphere is 2-dimensional, while the hypersphere's surface is 3-dimensional.

By the end of the nineteenth century, mathematicians had discovered a wealth of finite spaces without boundaries. In 1900, German astronomer Karl Schwarzschild (1873–1916) brought these ideas to the astronomical community. His main example was the 3-torus, which you study in Lesson 6.

Stars and Galaxies

Each star you see at night is a sun similar to our own. Stars are not spread evenly throughout space but are clustered into galaxies. The galaxy we live in is called the Milky Way. We see nearby stars in the Milky Way as individual stars, but the remaining stars in the Milky Way are so numerous and so distant that we see them as a splotchy white band extending across the sky. The next time you look at the sky on a clear night, with no moon and away from city lights, you will see the Milky Way clearly. At first you may think it's a stray white cloud stretching across the sky, but it's not. It's our galaxy. It got the name Milky Way because it looks like spilled milk.

The Andromeda galaxy, which you can see as a small white smudge in the direction of the constellation Andromeda, is the only other galaxy visible to the naked eye. Using the Hubble Space Telescope, we can see roughly one hundred billion other galaxies. Each, like our Milky Way, is an island of stars.

Andromeda galaxy

The Expansion of the Universe

In 1915, Albert Einstein (1879–1955) found a geometric explanation of gravity (his famous Theory of General Relativity). By 1917, he was surprised to find that his theory was incompatible with a universe of constant size. In 1922, Russian mathematician Alexander Friedmann (1888–1925) realized that Einstein's theory predicted an expanding universe, but the common belief in an unchanging universe was so strong that not even Einstein could accept this conclusion. Nevertheless, Friedmann's prediction was quickly confirmed. By 1929, astronomers observed that light reaching us from distant galaxies gets "stretched out" along the way, providing evidence that space itself expands during the billions of years the light spends traveling from a distant galaxy to us.

To understand how space expands, imagine 3-tori of different sizes (see the figure at the top of the next page). The penultimate 3-torus represents the modern universe. Because the universe is expanding, it will be bigger in the future. Conversely, the universe was smaller in the past. If we look roughly 10 to 15 billion years into the past, the universe had zero size. This was the time of the Big Bang, the birth of the universe.

Reading (continued)

Not drawn to scale

Big Bang	Infant universe	Past universe	Modern universe	Future universe
0 years	100,000 years	1 billion years	10 billion years	20 billion years

The early universe was small but very hot, because its matter and energy were compressed into a tiny volume. For the first 300,000 years, all of space was filled with a material similar to the outer layers of the modern sun. The radiation remaining from the hot, young universe is still observable today. But because the universe has been expanding, waves that were once visible light have been stretched out to become microwaves. The detection of this microwave background radiation in 1965 provided direct evidence in support of the hot Big Bang explanation for the birth of the universe.

New Understanding

Just as paleontologists use fossils to learn the history of life on Earth, cosmologists use the microwave background radiation to learn about the universe. Exactly how old is the universe? Is it flat or curved? Is it finite or infinite? How did the galaxies form?

In 1998–1999, scientists in the BOOMERANG project (Balloon Observations of Millimetric Extragalactic Radiation and Geophysics) used a balloon to carry microwave detectors to an altitude of 37 kilometers to measure the microwave background radiation in a portion of the sky over Antarctica. Their initial results, released in April 2000, provide tentative evidence that space is flat, not curved. That is, the universe could be like an infinite flat plane or it could be like the flat 2-torus on which you played the computer games in Lessons 4 and 5, but it cannot be curved like a sphere. More precisely, the real universe could be an infinite 3-dimensional space, or it could be a finite 3-torus (or any one of the spaces you will see in Lesson 9), but it cannot be Riemann's hypersphere unless the hypersphere is so huge that we are seeing only a tiny portion of it. A tiny portion

Reading (continued)

of Riemann's hypersphere would look approximately flat in the same way that a tiny portion of Earth's spherical surface—for example, the surface of the ice on a frozen lake—looks approximately flat.

To confirm BOOMERANG's observation of an approximately flat universe, in the spring of 2001, NASA (National Aeronautics and Space Administration) will launch the Microwave Anisotropy Probe, which will make detailed measurements of the full sky, providing preliminary data by early 2002 and full data by 2003.

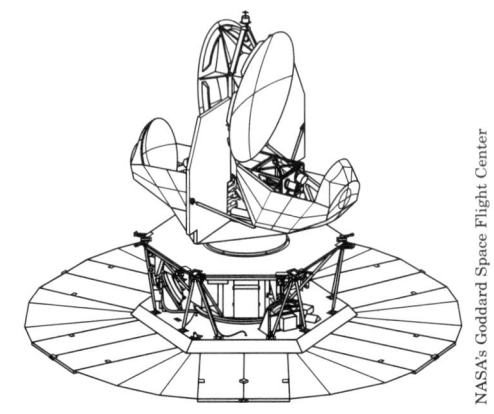

Microwave Anisotropy Probe

Resources for Further Study

1. Folger, T. "The Magnificent Mission." *Discover,* May 2000.

2. Luminet, J. P., G. Starkman, and J. Weeks. "Is Space Finite?" *Scientific American,* April 1999.

3. Osserman, R. *Poetry of the Universe.* New York: Anchor Books, 1996.

4. Check your library for books on cosmology and its history; or check science sites on the Internet, such as Amazing Space (**http://amazing-space.stsci.edu/**). You can find beautiful pictures of galaxies at **http://oposite.stsci.edu/pubinfo/pr.html** and **http://www.smv.org/hastings/galaxy.htm**.

5. You can find more information about BOOMERANG on their Web site at **http://www.physics.ucsb.edu/~boomerang**.

Reading (continued)

Questions

1. Did Leucippus and Democritus think space was finite or infinite?

2. Did Aristotle and his followers think space was finite or infinite? Did they think space had a boundary?

3. For the 2,000-year period from 400 B.C. to A.D. 1600, how did most Europeans imagine the universe?

4. What astronomical evidence helped convince sixteenth- and seventeenth-century philosophers to reject Aristotle's model of a finite universe in favor of an infinite one?

5. Who first proposed a universe that is finite yet has no boundary? Describe the universe he proposed.

6. When Karl Schwarzschild shared with astronomers the possibility of a finite universe with no boundary, what example did he use?

7. What is a galaxy?

8. What is the name of the galaxy we live in? Why did it get this name?

9. How many other galaxies can we see with the naked eye? How many other galaxies can we see with telescopes?

10. Who applied Einstein's theory of gravity to arrive at the surprising prediction that space is expanding?

11. What evidence confirms that space is expanding?

12. Approximately how old is the universe?

13. What was the universe like during its first 300,000 years?

14. The early universe glowed with visible light as bright as the sun. The light from that period still fills the modern universe but has been stretched out to become microwaves instead of visible light. What stretched the light?

15. Fossils are to paleontology as _____ is to cosmology.

Reading: Celestial Map

Locating the Andromeda Galaxy

This star chart shows that for observers at latitudes similar to that of the continental United States, the Andromeda galaxy is nearly overhead at 11 P.M. on October 1, at 10 P.M. on November 1, at 8 P.M. on December 1, and at 6 P.M. on January 1.

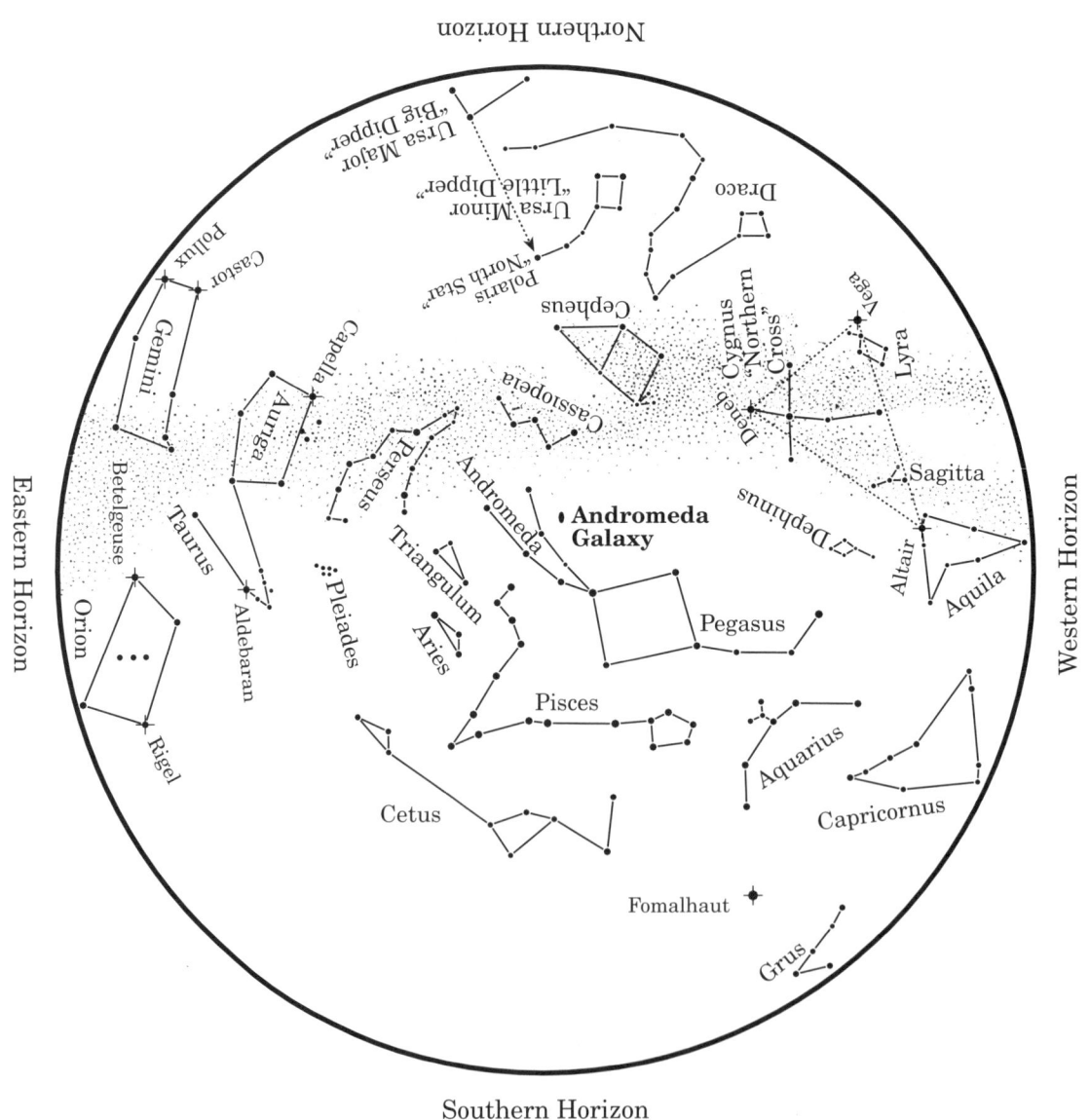

68 The 3-Torus

Exploring the Shape of Space
©2001 Key Curriculum Press

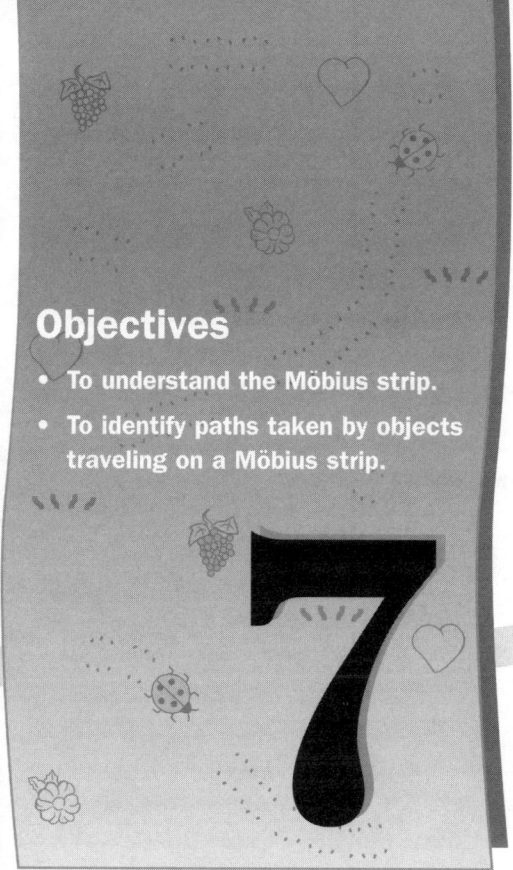

Möbius Strips

Objectives

- To understand the Möbius strip.
- To identify paths taken by objects traveling on a Möbius strip.

Materials

Plain 8.5-by-11-inch or 8.5-by-14-inch paper (one sheet per student)

Scissors

Tape or glue

Transparency 7a: Möbius Tic-Tac-Toe (optional)

Transparency 7b: Tic-Tac-Toe Tiling View (optional)

Activity 7a: Making Möbius Strips

Activity 7b: Möbius Strip Tiling View

Homework 7: Möbius Strips

Outline

Location: classroom

20 minutes: Making Möbius Strips (Activity 7a; groups)

15 minutes: Möbius Tic-Tac-Toe (whole class)

20 minutes: Möbius Strip Tiling View (Activity 7b; groups)

Vocabulary

Möbius strip

Teacher Notes

Activities

Making Möbius Strips

Have students complete Activity 7a. As they work, circulate about the room monitoring their progress, asking and answering questions. As students finish the first part of Question 6, ask them this bonus question:

How many twists are in the cylinder?

There are two full twists.

Try to reassemble the original Möbius strip from the twisted cylinder.

This is harder than it looks.

Möbius Tic-Tac-Toe

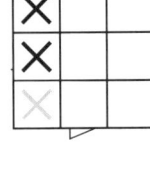

On the chalkboard, draw a tic-tac-toe board on a virtual Möbius strip, and draw two Xs as shown at left. Or use Transparency 7a and have a pen ready to mark additional moves.

Where can X move to win?

The students will probably suggest the lower left.

What if that spot is blocked by an O?

The lower right is also a win for X!

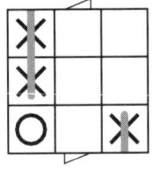

It might be helpful to put letters or colored dots above and below each column to show the gluing.

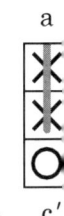

Play a game or two of Möbius tic-tac-toe as a class. As with cylindrical tic-tac-toe, divide the class into two teams. Have each team send a representative to the board to mark the team's moves. The representative does not select the move but merely records the team's consensus.

Let students choose partners and play another couple of games on scrap paper at their seats.

Möbius Strip Tiling View

Have students complete Activity 7b. If possible, check students' answers to Question 2 before they proceed to Question 3. Moreover, before students play the games in Question 3 at their seats, you may first want the class to form two teams and play a game or two

Teacher Notes

in the tiling view on the chalkboard or on Transparency 7b. Emphasize that whenever a student makes a move, she or he immediately marks all its images. After students have played a game or two as a class, let them play the games in Question 3 at their seats as you circulate about the room checking that they are correctly marking all the images of each move.

Homework

Distribute Homework 7, due tomorrow.

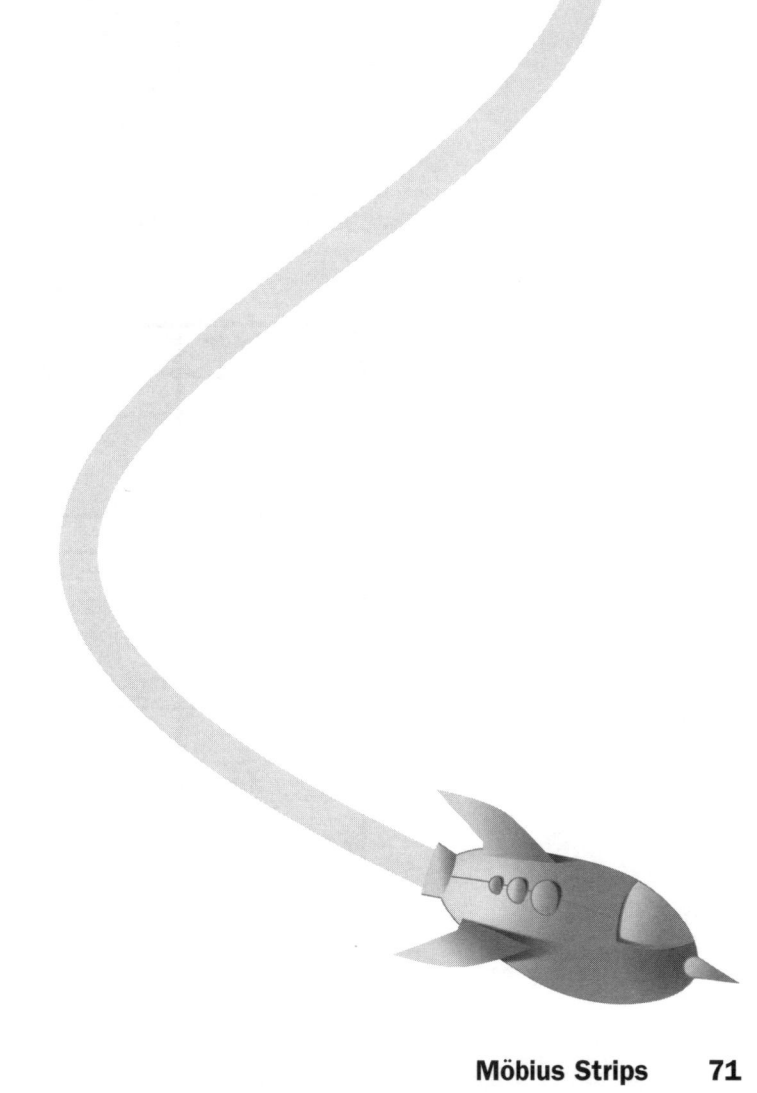

Möbius Tic-Tac-Toe

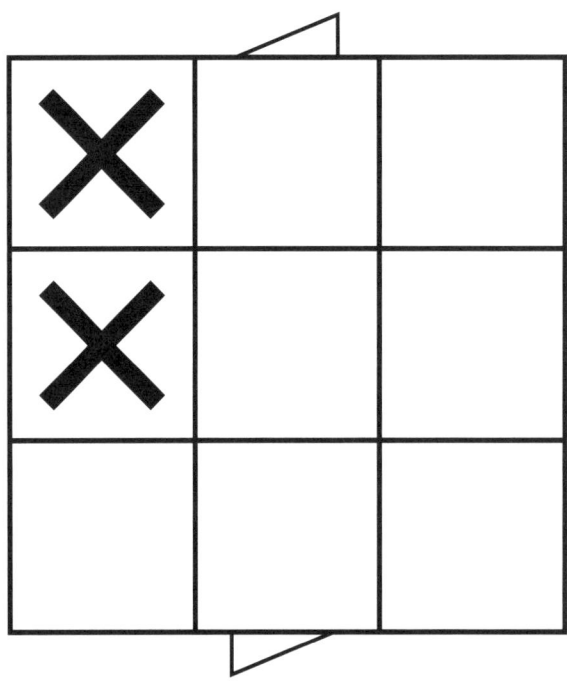

Transparency 7b

Tic-Tac-Toe Tiling View

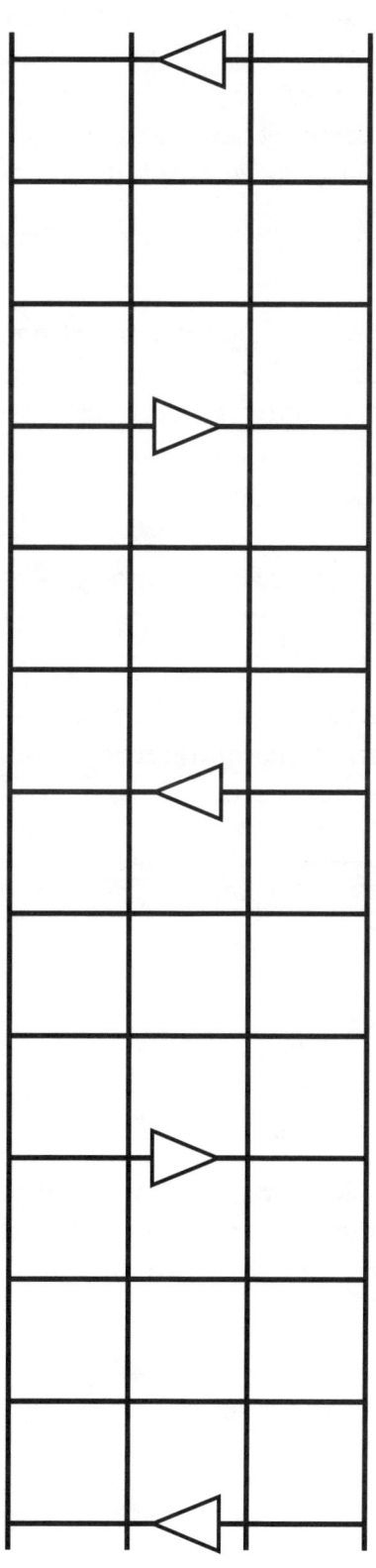

Möbius Strips

Activity 7a   Name_____

Making Möbius Strips

1. Cut a blank sheet of 8.5-by-11-inch paper into four strips, each about 2 by 11 inches. (8.5-by-14-inch paper is even better.) Make one strip into a cylinder by taping the ends with no twist, as shown at left, and make a second strip into a Möbius strip by taping the ends together with a half twist (a twist through 180 degrees), as shown at right.

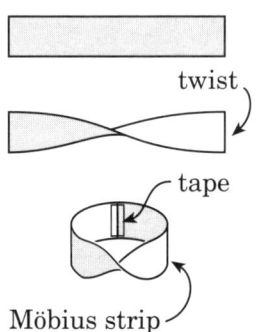

2. Mark an **X** somewhere on your cylinder. Starting at the **X**, draw a line down the center of the strip until you return to the starting point. Do the same for the Möbius strip. What happens?

3. The first figure below shows a gluing diagram for a cylinder. Mark arrows on the second figure to make a gluing diagram for a Möbius strip.

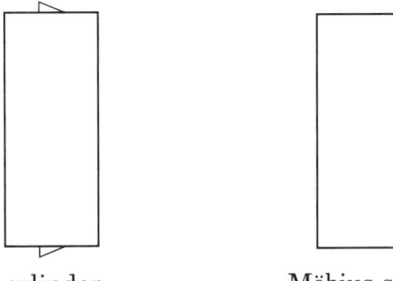

cylinder   Möbius strip

To check your answer, ask yourself what would happen if you stretched the rectangle around to glue the top and bottom so that the arrows matched. Would you get a Möbius strip?

Activity 7a (continued)   Name _____

4. The gluing diagram you created in Question 3 defines a virtual Möbius strip, which is a little different from a paper Möbius strip. A paper Möbius strip has a slight thickness and occupies a small volume; there is a small separation between its "two" sides. The virtual Möbius strip has zero thickness; it is truly 2-dimensional. Mark an **X** on the virtual Möbius strip at right and trace down the centerline; you'll get back to your starting point after only one trip around!

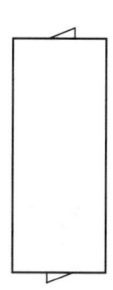

5. A cylinder has two boundary circles. How many boundary circles does a Möbius strip have?

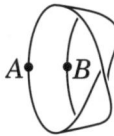 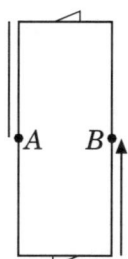

   (Hint: If an ant starts walking north from point *A*, what happens?)

6. a. Take a pair of scissors and cut your paper Möbius strip down its centerline. What do you get?

   b. Take the result from the previous step and cut down its centerline. What do you get now?

Exploring the Shape of Space **Möbius Strips**

Activity 7b   Name _____

Möbius Strip Tiling View

1. The Möbius strip tiling view is similar to the 2-torus tiling view you explored in the computer games in Lesson 5, but there are two differences.

   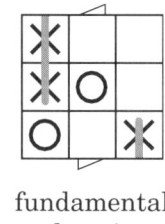
   fundamental domain

   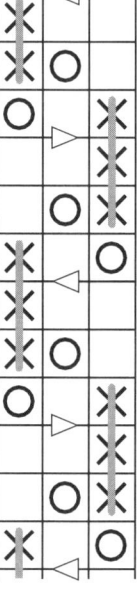
   tiling view

   a. Why does the Möbius strip tiling extend vertically but not horizontally?

   b. In the Möbius strip tiling, why are alternate images mirror-reversed?

2. Try a game.

   a. Find a partner and play a game of Möbius tic-tac-toe in the fundamental domain below.

   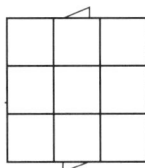

   b. Draw the tiling view of your game in the space at right.

   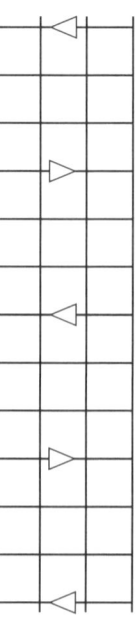

3. Find a partner and play several games of Möbius tic-tac-toe directly in the tiling views on the following page. Each time you make a move, be sure to mark all its images in the tiling view.

76   Möbius Strips   Exploring the Shape of Space
                                                                 ©2001 Key Curriculum Press

Activity 7b (continued)   Name_____

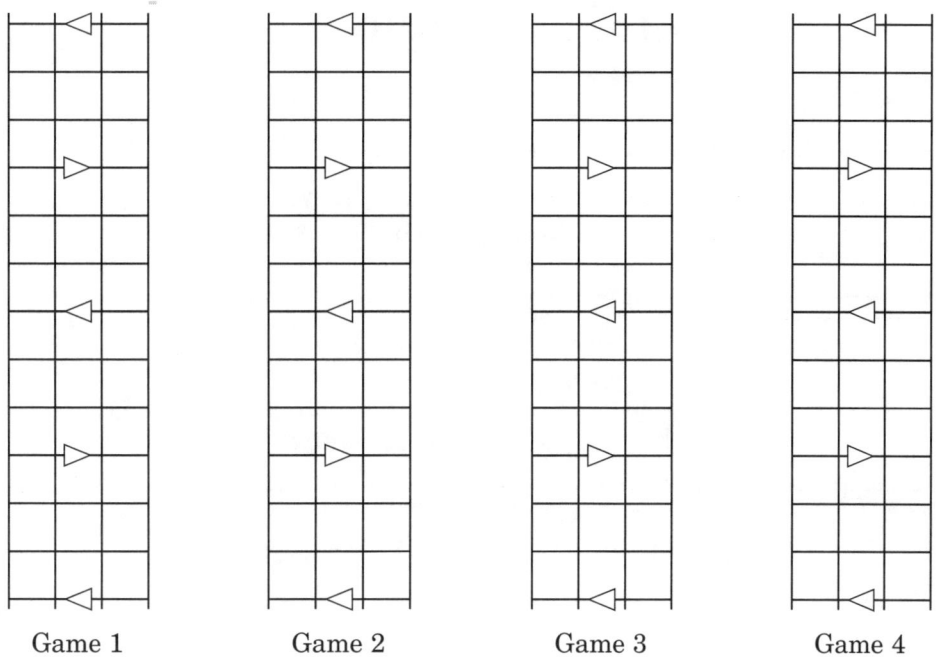

Game 1   Game 2   Game 3   Game 4

Bonus Problem

You might imagine a Möbius strip to have a "seam" where the fundamental domain's top and bottom edges meet. But you can also imagine a Möbius strip with no seam. Play a few games of Möbius tic-tac-toe in the tiling view of a seamless Möbius strip. As usual, whenever you make a move, be sure to draw all its images.

seam

seamless

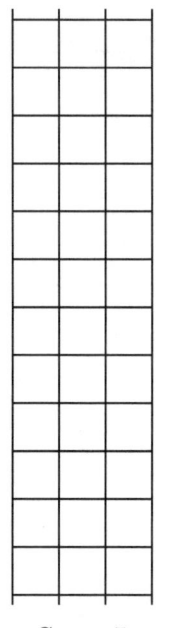 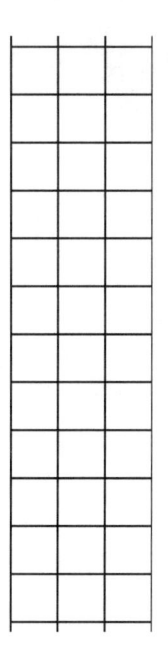 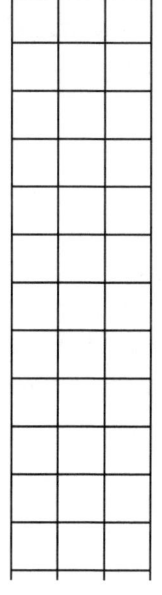 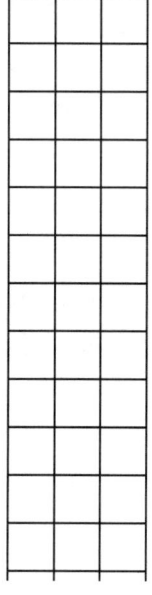

Game 5   Game 6   Game 7   Game 8

Exploring the Shape of Space **Möbius Strips**
©2001 Key Curriculum Press

Homework 7

Möbius Strips

1. Make a long, skinny rectangle (about 2 by 11 inches) as you did in class. Crease it to divide it into thirds lengthwise, and then tape the ends to make a Möbius strip.

    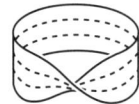

   a. What do you think will happen when you cut your Möbius strip along the creases? Write your prediction here.

   b. Get a pair of scissors and cut along the creases. Describe the results of your experiment here, and include your cut-up Möbius strip when you turn in your homework.

   c. Color in this virtual Möbius strip using a different color for each of the pieces your paper Möbius strip fell into when you cut it.

   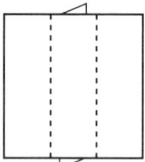

2. The three flatlanders Alex, Bobbie, and Chris line up for a race on a virtual Möbius strip racetrack. All three run due north at exactly the same speed. Which flatlander will return to his or her own starting point first?

   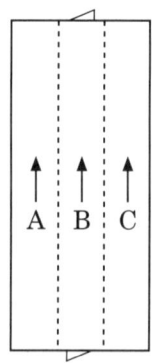

78   **Möbius Strips**

Exploring the Shape of Space
©2001 Key Curriculum Press

Homework 7 (continued)

Bonus Problem

Are these two first moves equivalent in Möbius tic-tac-toe? Explain.

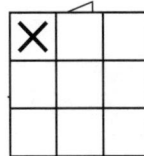 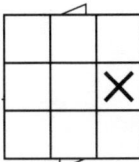

Objectives

- To develop a deep intuitive understanding of the Klein bottle as a finite universe with no boundary.
- To see how the Klein bottle's mirror-reversing properties distinguish it from the torus.
- To learn to trace paths accurately through a Klein bottle universe.

Klein Bottle Games

Materials

Computers with Java-capable Web browsers (one computer for every two students is ideal)

Torus Games Web pages (on CD-ROM and available online)

Transparency 8: Klein Bottle Games Introduction (optional)

Activity 8: Games on a Klein Bottle

Homework 8: Klein Bottle Games

Outline

Location: computer lab

5 minutes: Introduction (whole class)

30+ minutes: Games on a Klein Bottle (Activity 8, and computer games)

Vocabulary

Klein bottle

glide reflection axis (older grades only)

Teacher Notes

Activities

Introduction

This quick introduction presents the Klein bottle. Ask students to direct their attention to the projection system (if you have one) or gather around your monitor (if they all fit) or otherwise just follow along using their own computers as you show Transparency 8.

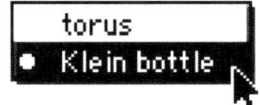

From the main page (**TorusGames/index.html**), click to the Introduction and use the pop-up menu to switch from **torus** mode to **Klein bottle** mode.

We're going to return to the computer games, but today you will play them in a new space called a *Klein bottle*. Side to side, the Klein bottle is like a cylinder.

Grab the flower with the mouse.

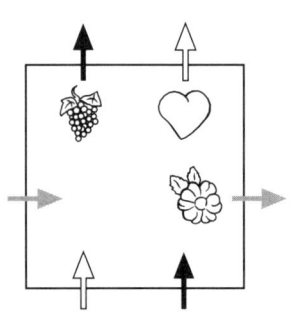

What do you think will happen if we drag the flower past the right edge of the square?

It will come back from the left.

Grab the grapes with the mouse.

Top to bottom, the Klein bottle is like a Möbius strip. Think back to the tic-tac-toe games you played on a Möbius strip. If we drag the grapes straight up, where will they come back?

They will come back at the bottom right.

Where will the heart come back if we drag it straight up?

At the bottom left.

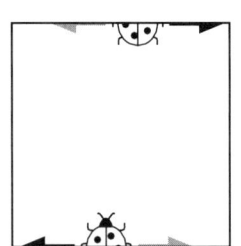

Position the ladybug to straddle the top and bottom edges, then slide her side to side so students can see what happens.

Return to the main page and click to the tic-tac-toe game. Use the menu to the right of the tic-tac-toe board to change from **torus** mode to **Klein bottle** mode and from **human vs. computer** mode to **human vs. human** mode.

 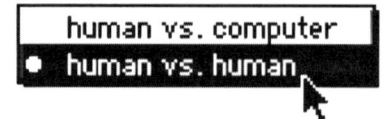

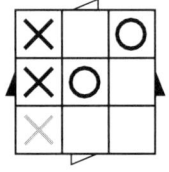

Begin a game with the four moves shown at left.

Where can X move to win?

Students will probably suggest the bottom left corner.

Click the **New Game** button to clear the board.

82   Klein Bottle Games   *Exploring the Shape of Space*

Teacher Notes

What if O got smarter and blocked X?

Make the four moves shown at right.

Where can X win now?

Students will probably suggest the bottom right corner.

Click the **New Game** button once more.

O is continuing to learn from experience, and the game goes like this.

Make the four moves shown at right.

Can X still win?

Send students to their computers to investigate! Don't give away the answer. This is the first question in Activity 8.

Games on a Klein Bottle

Pass out Activity 8 and circulate about the room answering students' questions and congratulating their successes. If they get stuck, ask questions to get them thinking, without revealing the answers. Make sure they switch to **Klein bottle** mode every time they change games.

If any students have trouble with Question 1a, suggest that they slowly scroll the board upward (drag with the right mouse button on a Windows computer or drag with the Command key held down on a Macintosh), and the answer will become obvious.

As students finish the activity sheet, they may play freely with the games for the rest of the class period. Remind them to switch from **torus** mode to **Klein bottle** mode whenever they change games. As in Lessons 4 and 5, have the students work in pairs, and suggest that they try both **human vs. human** mode and **human vs. computer** mode for the tic-tac-toe and chess games. As the students play, continue to circulate about the room asking and answering questions.

Homework

Distribute Homework 8, due tomorrow.

Students May Wonder, Where's the Bottle?

The torus can be stretched around to become a doughnut surface, but what about the Klein bottle? Surprisingly, analogous models of a Klein bottle must have self-intersections! Two such models appear on the following page. The self-intersections may be removed either by passing to 4-dimensional space or by passing to a different 3-dimensional space, for example, the half-turn space of Lesson 9.

Exploring the Shape of Space

Klein Bottle Games

Teacher Notes

However, for the reasons mentioned in the note at the end of Lesson 4, the flat Klein bottle is most important for cosmology and is therefore the topic of this lesson's games and activities.

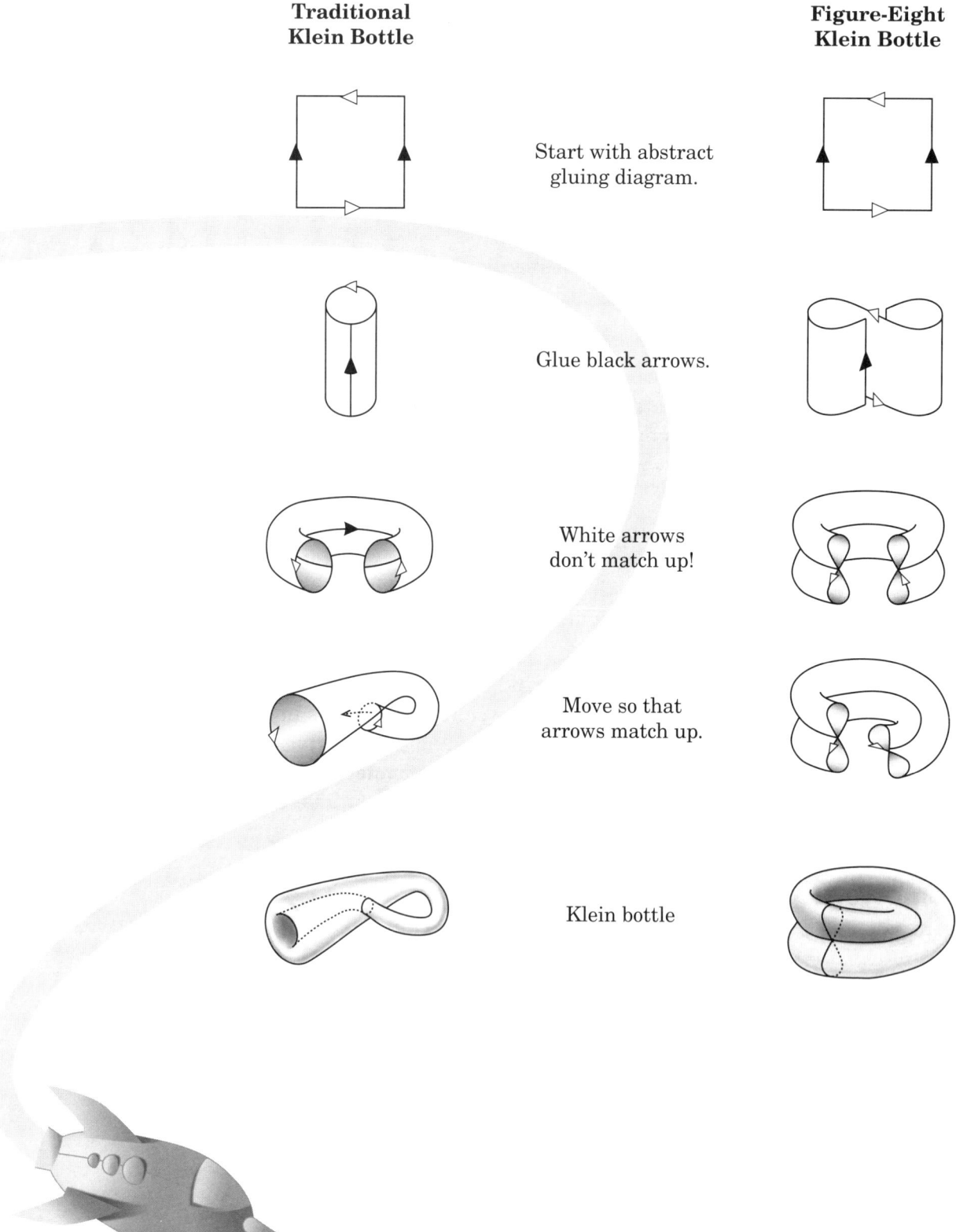

Klein Bottle Games Introduction

Transparency 8

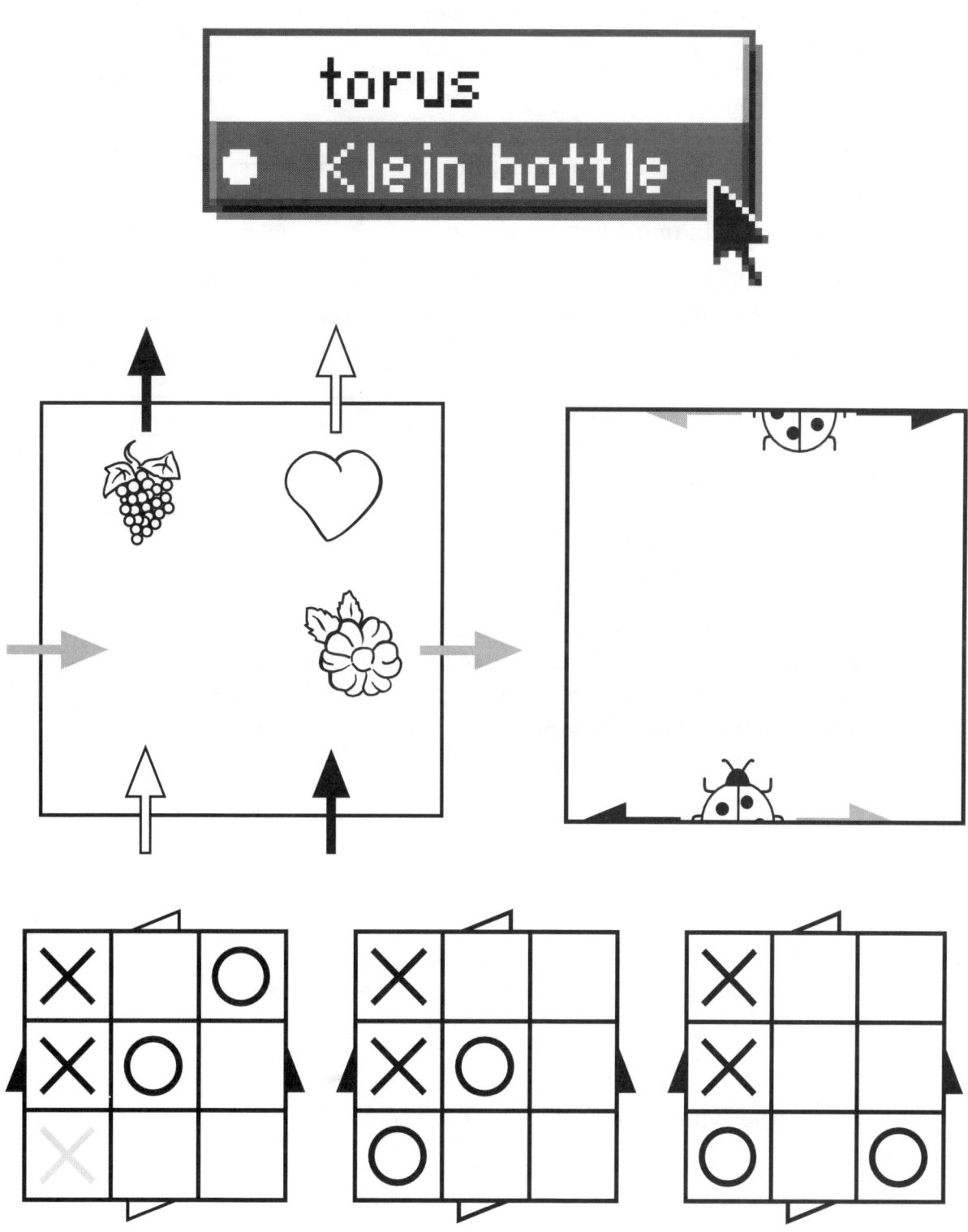

Exploring the Shape of Space
©2001 Key Curriculum Press

Klein Bottle Games   85

Activity 8   Name_____

Games on a Klein Bottle

1. Open the tic-tac-toe computer game. Switch from **torus** mode to **Klein bottle** mode and from **human vs. computer** mode to **human vs. human** mode. Set up the game shown at right.

   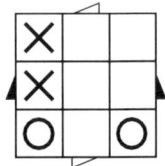

   a. Mark the square in the fundamental domain (shown above at the right) where **X** can win immediately.

   b. Draw the tiling view of this game in the grid at right, and put a line through **X**'s winning three-in-a-row. (The tic-tac-toe computer game won't draw the tiling view for you, but you can scroll up, down, and sideways to deduce what the tiling view should look like.)

   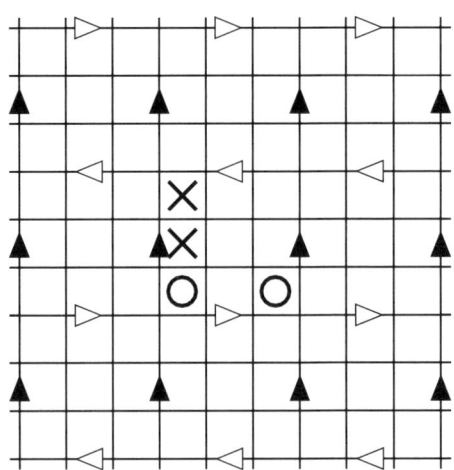

2. Open the maze computer game and switch from **torus** mode to **Klein bottle** mode.

   a. Find a way to drag the mouse past the top of the board so he comes back at the bottom. Look at him very closely before and after. How is he different? (Not just his position, but his body.) Why does this happen?

   b. Drag the mouse past the left side of the board so he comes back at the right. Look at him very closely before and after. Has he changed?

   c. What is the significance of the dotted green lines?

86   Klein Bottle Games   Exploring the Shape of Space
                                             ©2001 Key Curriculum Press

Activity 8 (continued)   Name_____

3. Open the jigsaw computer game, switch from **torus** mode to **Klein bottle** mode, and set the puzzle size to **3 × 3**. Assemble the puzzle except for the last piece.

   a. Does it look as if the last piece would fit into the remaining hole? (Don't put it in yet!)

   b. Being careful not to let the piece fall into the hole, slide it past the top edge of the board so it comes back at the bottom. Now does it look as if the last piece would fit into the hole?

   c. If you slid the piece past the top of the board 4317 more times, would it fit into the hole? Explain.

4. Go to the first Klein bottle word search puzzle (the one with people's names).

   a. The first two letters in the name "Albert" are shown in the first Klein bottle below. Find the rest of the name in the puzzle, and copy it.

   b. How would the name "Albert" look on a torus if the name started at the same place? Write it in the second puzzle.

   c. Why does the name "Albert" change direction (from southeast to southwest) when it crosses the bottom/top edge of the Klein bottle fundamental domain?

   d. Find the name "Christopher" and copy it in the third puzzle.

   e. What would happen to the name "Christopher" on a torus?

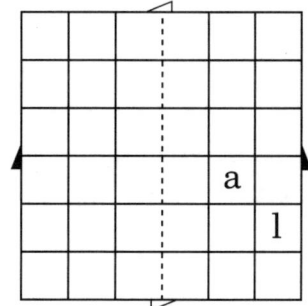
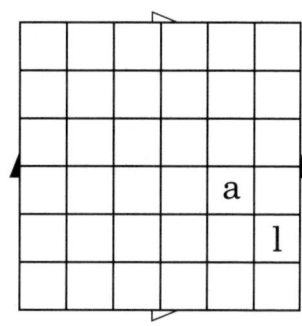
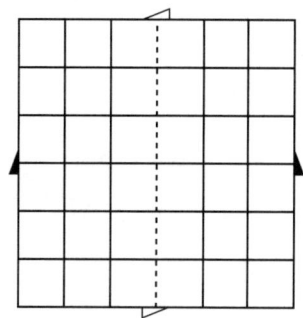

Exploring the Shape of Space **Klein Bottle Games**
©2001 Key Curriculum Press

Homework 8

Klein Bottle Games

1. Find all winning locations for **X** in the Klein bottle tic-tac-toe game shown here. (Hint: Draw the tiling view of the game.)

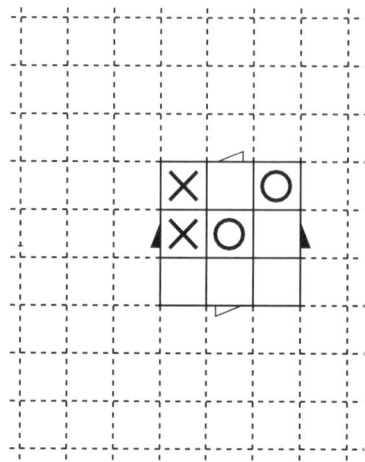

2. Make your own Klein bottle word search puzzle. You may either design it on a piece of scrap paper or use the word search editor provided with the computer games. The more words you fit in, the better. Include at least one word of seven letters or more. Be sure to provide a list of your hidden words.

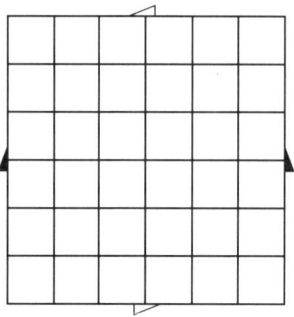

Word list
1.
2.
3.
4.
5.
6.
7.
8.

3. In class you saw that a Klein bottle has two special lines of symmetry, which are marked with dotted green lines in the Klein bottle maze game.

   a. When the mouse goes past the top of the board just to the left of a symmetry line, where does he come back?

   b. When the mouse goes past the top of the board just to the right of a symmetry line, where does he come back?

   c. When the mouse goes past the top of the board exactly on a symmetry line, where does he come back?

Homework 8 (continued)   Name _____

4. The ladybug in the Klein bottle at right walks in a straight line until she returns to her starting point. Draw her path.

   (Hint 1: If you are unsure what happens when the ladybug crosses the top edge of the square, try drawing the tiling view on a separate sheet of paper.)

   (Hint 2: Think back to the name "Albert" in the word search puzzle you did in class.)

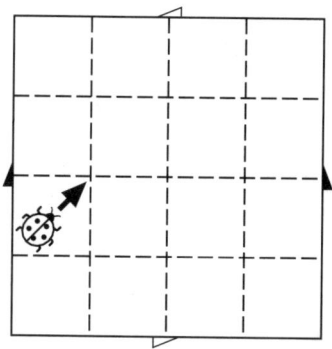

Bonus Problems

1. Create your own Klein bottle crossword puzzle. You may either design it on a piece of paper or use the crossword puzzle editor provided with the computer games.

2. Mark a fundamental domain on this tiling view of a Klein bottle jigsaw puzzle.

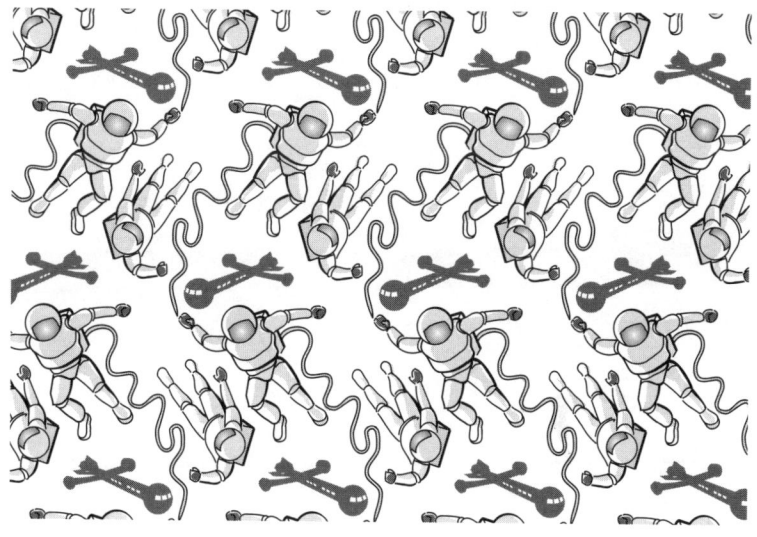

3. Can a word intersect itself (at right angles) in a Klein bottle word search? How does the intersection in a 5-by-5 Klein bottle differ from that in a 6-by-6 Klein bottle? Try it!

Exploring the Shape of Space   **Klein Bottle Games**
©2001 Key Curriculum Press

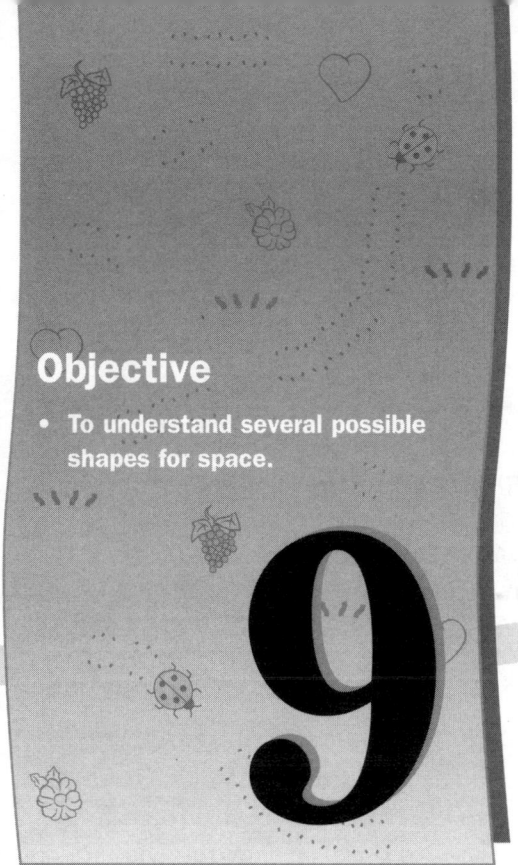

Objective
- To understand several possible shapes for space.

9 More Shapes for Space

Materials

4 sheets of construction paper, each a different color

Scissors

Tape or glue

The Shape of Space video and VCR

Video Guide 2: *The Shape of Space,* Part 2

Computer games in the 3-torus and other 3-dimensional spaces (optional, available from **www.keypress.com/space/**)

Activity 9: Mystery Spaces (one activity sheet and one of each mystery space per group plus extra copies of Mystery Space 1)

Homework 9: More Shapes for Space

Outline

Location: classroom

15 minutes: *The Shape of Space* video

20 minutes: Mystery Spaces (Activity 9; groups)

5 minutes: What Do We See? (whole class)

10 minutes: Tiling View

5 minutes: The Real Universe

15 minutes: 3-Dimensional Computer Games (optional)

Vocabulary

Klein space

quarter-turn space

half-turn space

Teacher Notes

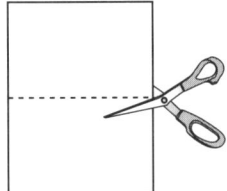

Preparation

Before class, get four sheets of construction paper of different colors, cut each sheet horizontally in half, as shown at left, and reassemble the pieces to form two identical four-color rectangles like the one at right. Attach one four-color rectangle to the center of the front wall of the classroom (on the chalkboard if necessary), and the other four-color rectangle to the point directly opposite on the back wall of the classroom. Position the rectangles so that corresponding colors are directly opposite each other (blue opposite blue, red opposite red, and so on) as shown below.

Activities

The Shape of Space Video

Read, display, or distribute copies of the questions on Video Guide 2. Show the entire eleven-minute video *The Shape of Space* including the first half, which was shown in Lesson 6. After showing the video, discuss the answers to the questions on the video guide and any questions the students may have. (Following *The Shape of Space* is a nine-minute interview with the author. Show the interview on the day you give the test.)

Mystery Spaces

Have students complete Activity 9, while you circulate about the room helping them to understand the gluings and to visualize the spaces.

What Do We See?

Make sure the four-color rectangles are attached to the centers of the front and back classroom walls, as explained in the Preparation section. Ask students to imagine the space inside the classroom as a 3-torus and to visualize the repeating images they would see. The view is similar to the fly-through scenes in the video and in any case should be familiar to students from Lesson 6.

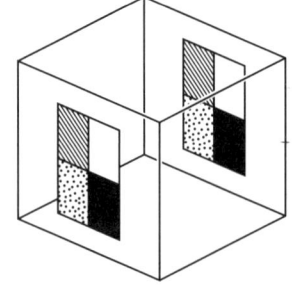

Turn one of the colored sheets over and retape it to the wall as shown in the diagram. The two side walls, as well as the floor and ceiling, remain glued as in the 3-torus, that is, straight across.

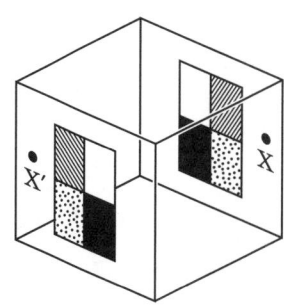

If a student walks through the front wall at point X, where does she come back?

At point X'.

When students look forward in this space, what do they see?

They see themselves from behind.

How does the view differ from the view in the 3-torus?

Here the students see a mirror image of the classroom, reversed right to left. This is because when their line of sight leaves at the front right, it returns at the back left, and vice versa.

This space (already introduced in Activity 8) is called the **Klein space,** because it is a solid version of the flat Klein bottle the students played with in Lesson 8. The second space in the video is also a Klein space. The only difference is that in the video the spaceship comes back with a top-to-bottom reversal, instead of a left-to-right reversal as illustrated here.

If time permits, you may continue the discussion of the Klein space to consider its mirror-reversal effect.

What happens to a person who walks through the front wall at its exact center?

She comes back at the exact center of the back wall, but with her left arm where her right arm used to be and vice versa.

What happens if she tries to shake hands with another student?

She holds out her right hand, which looks like a left hand to the rest of the class. Shaking hands is difficult!

If she then writes her name on the chalkboard—in what she considers to be the standard left-to-right direction—how will it appear to the rest of the class?

The rest of the class will perceive it as running right to left.

How will the rest of the class's writing appear to her?

Also backward.

What if she takes a second trip through the front wall?

She gets reversed again, thereby restoring herself to her original condition.

Exploring the Shape of Space

Teacher Notes

Tiling View

Challenge the class to construct (a portion of) the tiling view for the *quarter-turn space,* using the paper fundamental domains each group constructed during Activity 9. That is, have the various groups pool their fundamental domains for the quarter-turn space and work together as a class to build a single tiling view. (Make sure that no fundamental domains for other spaces get mixed in accidentally!) The result will look like a stack of blocks—a "cubical packing." Each cube should touch its neighbors so that the markings match up exactly. If time permits, ask every student to construct another copy of the quarter-turn space's fundamental domain so the class can assemble a much larger portion of the tiling view.

With older students, discuss the tiling view's structure using the language of transformations. Neighboring cubes differ by a pure translation in two of the directions, but in the remaining direction, neighbors differ by a corkscrew motion—a translation composed with a 90-degree rotation.

What do inhabitants of the quarter-turn space see when they look in the direction of the square symbol?

They see another copy of their space, rotated 90 degrees.

What do they see beyond that image of their space?

They see another image of their space, but this one is rotated 180 degrees. It's upside down!

How far do they have to look to see a right-side-up image of their space?

To the fourth image. The first image is rotated 90 degrees, the second is rotated 180 degrees, the third is rotated 270 degrees, and the fourth is right side up again.

The Real Universe

How could we tell whether the real universe is a 3-torus, a Klein space, a quarter-turn space, or a *half-turn space?*

Let students discuss their ideas. They may suggest looking for repeating patterns in the galaxies, analogous to the repeating images of the classroom or the paper cubes discussed earlier in the lesson. The presence of reflections or rotations in the pattern of the galaxies would give a clue to the shape of the universe.

For up-to-date information on observations of the real universe, please see **http://www.keypress.com/space/**.

Teacher Notes

3-Dimensional Computer Games

The Web site **http://www.keypress.com/space/** offers 3-dimensional versions of some of the Torus and Klein Bottle Games, along with suggested classroom activities. You may wish to have students play the games and complete the activities to deepen their understanding of the spaces introduced in this lesson.

Homework

Distribute Homework 9, due tomorrow.

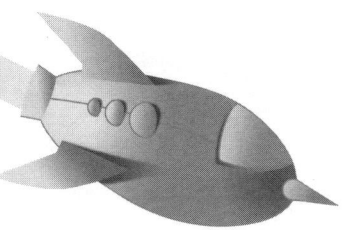

Video Guide 2

The Shape of Space, Part 2

The video shows two 3-dimensional universes:

- The 3-torus (all faces glued straight across)

- The Klein space (one pair of faces glued with a flip)

1. Are these spaces finite or infinite?

2. Do they have a boundary?

3. When the passengers in the spaceship look around, can they tell which of the two spaces they are traveling in? If so, how?

4. Could the real universe be a 3-torus or a Klein space?

Activity 9   Name_____

Mystery Spaces

Mystery Space 1	
Mystery Space 2	
Mystery Space 3	
Mystery Space 4	

Your group should assemble one copy of each of the four mystery spaces. To assemble each space, cut out the template, crease along all the fold lines, and tape or glue to assemble a cube. Make sure the markings appear on the outside. Each cube is the fundamental domain for a space. Imagine yourself to be a small person living inside.

1. Each cube's opposite faces are glued so that the markings match exactly. Decide which of the four mystery spaces is a *3-torus,* and write "3-torus" in the correct position in the table above. (Note: Here we mean that opposite faces are abstractly glued, in the sense that anything leaving through one face returns from the opposite face. Please don't try to attach opposite faces with real glue!)

2. The second half of the video *The Shape of Space* showed the *Klein space,* in which the spaceship came back reversed top to bottom but not reversed side to side. Decide which of the four mystery spaces is a Klein space, and write "Klein space" in the correct position in the table above.

3. The *quarter-turn space* has two pairs of faces glued straight across, as in the 3-torus, but the third pair of faces is glued with a quarter turn so that a traveler passing through that face comes back to his or her starting point rotated by 90 degrees. Decide which of the four mystery spaces is a quarter-turn space, and write "quarter-turn space" in the correct position in the table above.

4. The *half-turn space* is similar to the quarter-turn space, except that a traveler passing through the special face comes back rotated by 180 degrees instead of 90 degrees. Is your last remaining mystery space a half-turn space? If so, write "half-turn space" in the remaining position in the table.

Exploring the Shape of Space
©2001 Key Curriculum Press

More Shapes for Space

Activity 9 (continued)

Mystery Space 1

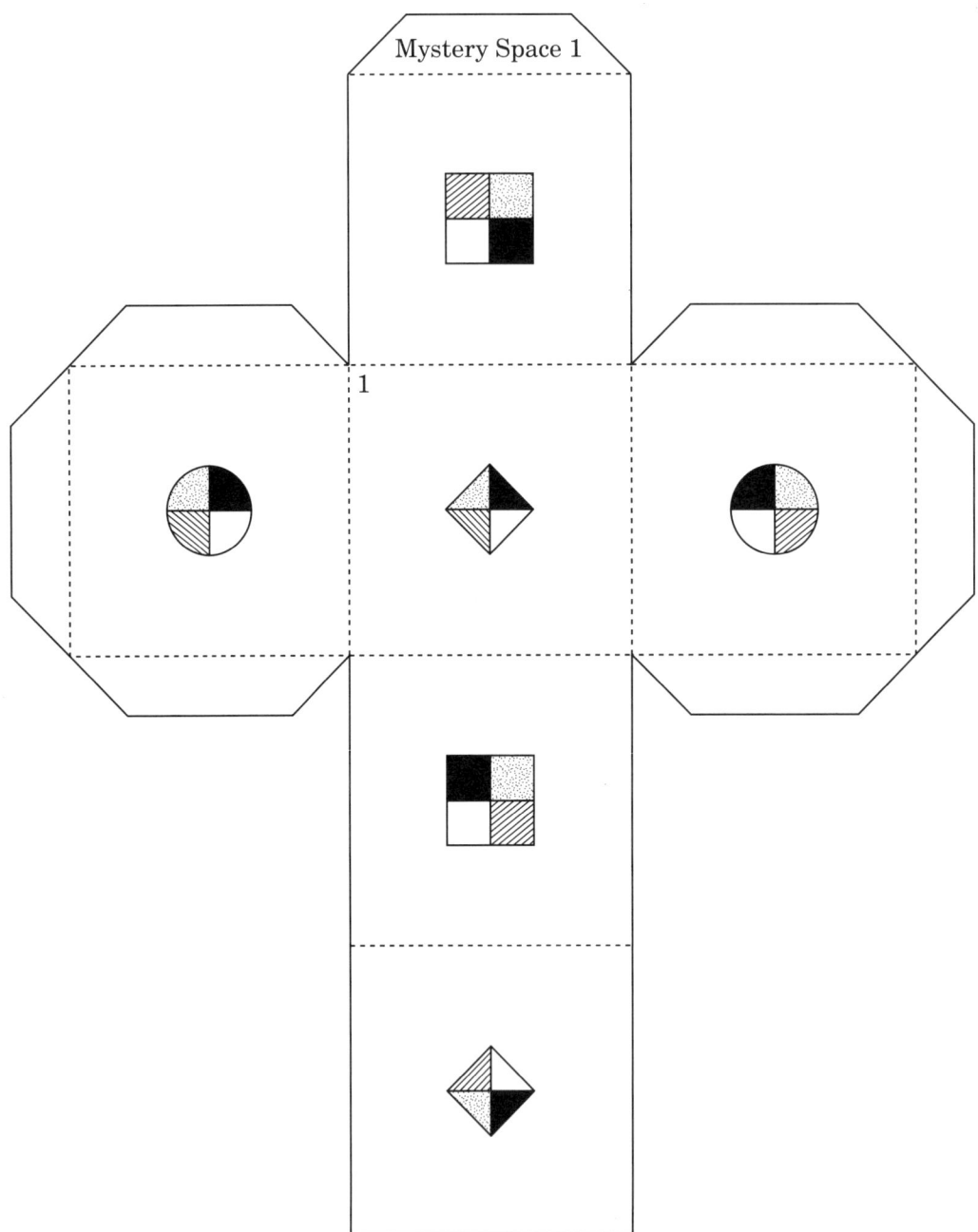

98 **More Shapes for Space**

Activity 9 (continued) Name_____

Mystery Space 2

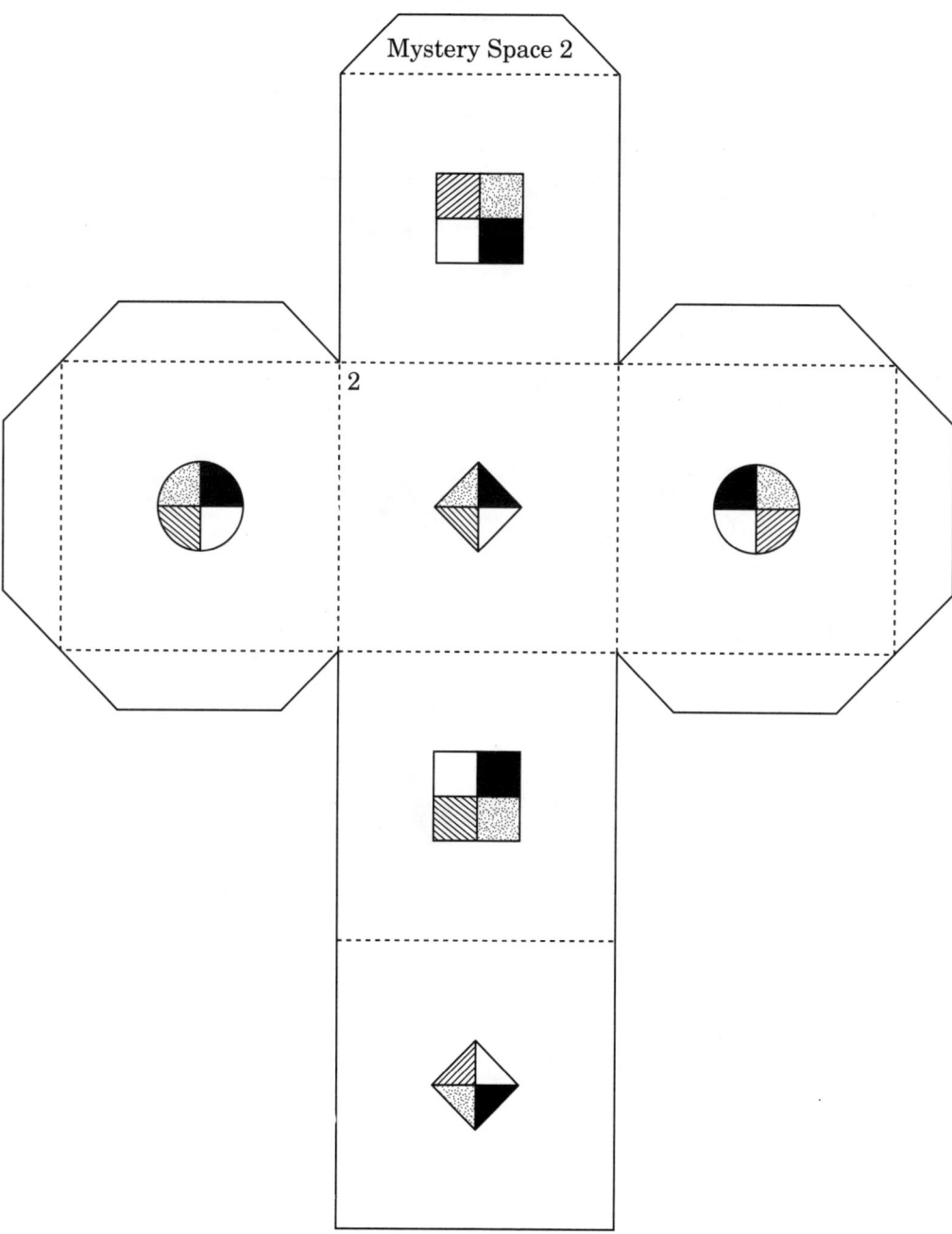

Exploring the Shape of Space
©2001 Key Curriculum Press

More Shapes for Space 99

Activity 9 (continued) Name_____

Mystery Space 3

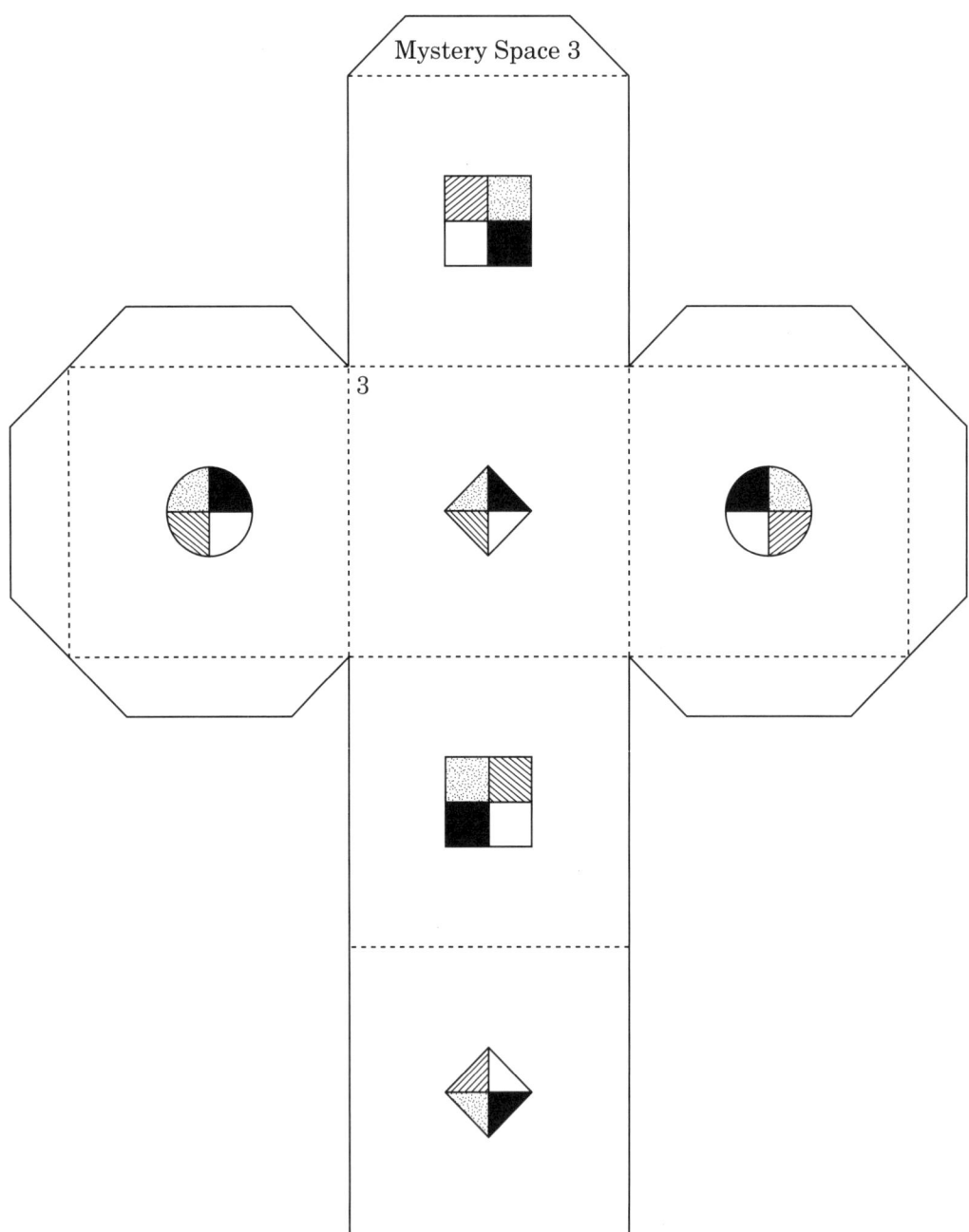

Activity 9 (continued)　　　　　　　　Name_____

Mystery Space 4

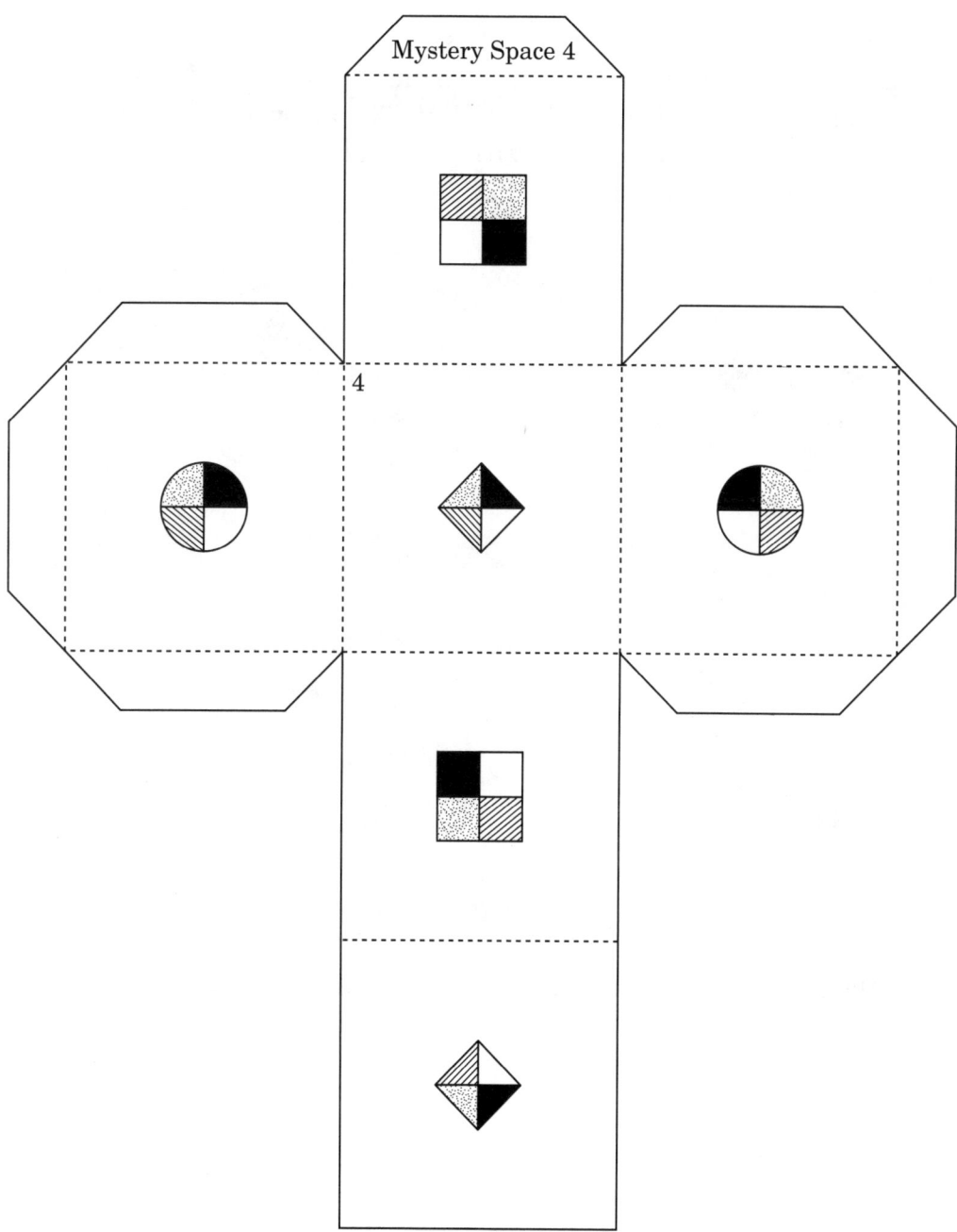

Exploring the Shape of Space
©2001 Key Curriculum Press

More Shapes for Space　101

Homework 9

More Shapes for Space

1. Write the name of each space whose fundamental domain appears below. Unmarked walls are glued to one another in the simple, straight-across way. (Hint: The answers are 3-torus, Klein space, quarter-turn space, and half-turn space, but not in that order.)

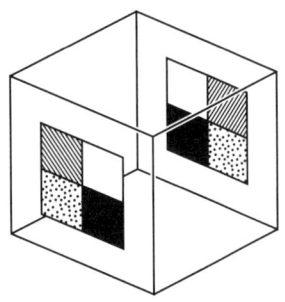
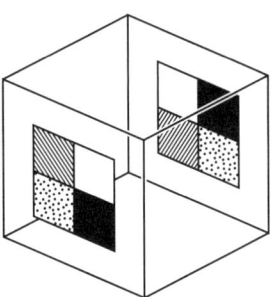

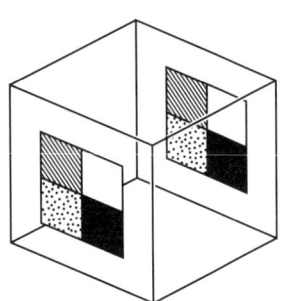
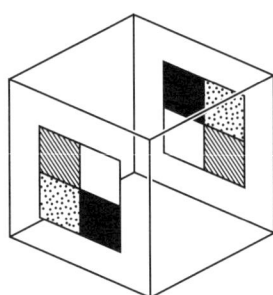

2. If the real universe were a quarter-turn space, how might we be able to tell?

Test

1. Mark **X**'s winning move in each game below. Note that the first two games are in a torus, while the second two are in a Klein bottle.

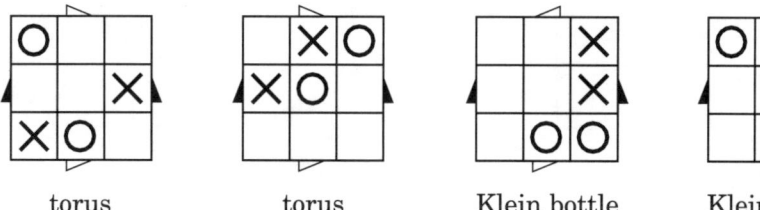

    torus   torus   Klein bottle   Klein bottle

2. The first figure below shows the fundamental domain view of a spaceship in a torus universe. Draw the tiling view. Do the same for the Klein bottle universe in the right-hand column below.

Torus	Klein bottle
Fundamental domain	**Fundamental domain**
Tiling view	**Tiling view**

Exploring the Shape of Space
©2001 Key Curriculum Press

Test (continued)   Name_____

3. A 2-dimensional torus universe contains the six planets shown below. Draw the shortest route from Zhur to Mhak.

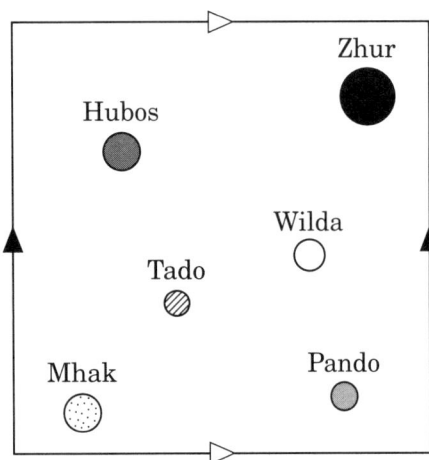

4. Draw an appropriate 1-dimensional universe in each box below.

	With boundary	**Without boundary**
Finite		
Infinite		

5. All but one of the following torus tic-tac-toe games are equivalent. Circle the one that's different.

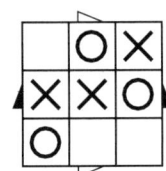 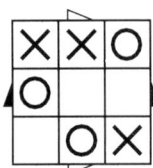 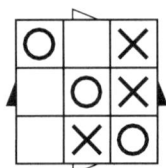 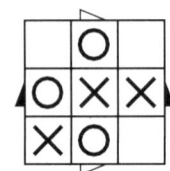

6. Is a 3-torus finite or infinite?

   Does it have a boundary?

   Is it 2-dimensional or 3-dimensional?

Test (continued)　　　　　　　　　　Name_____

7. What is the difference between a 2-torus and a 3-torus?

8. Could it be possible to see the same galaxy in two different directions in the sky? Explain your answer.

9. What is the difference between a cylinder and a Möbius strip?

10. Label the squares' edges to make a gluing diagram for each shape.

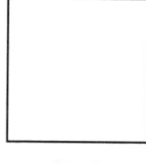　　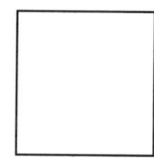　

　　cylinder　　　　　Möbius strip　　　　　torus　　　　　Klein bottle

11. Draw a plausible house in flatland. Show two flatlanders living in the house.

Answers

Activity 1: How Big Is the Universe?

1. 100,000,000,000 (11 zeros)
   Students familiar with scientific notation may prefer to write this number as 10^{11}.

2. 10,000,000,000,000,000,000,000 (22 zeros)
   Students familiar with scientific notation may prefer to write this number as 10^{22}. In words, it is ten sextillion.

3. Answers will vary. The purpose of this question is to get students thinking about whether or not the universe is infinite.

Homework 1: Flatland

1. Look for signs that students understand what it means to be confined to two dimensions. Eyes should not be inside the head, where light wouldn't reach them. The mouth must reach the outside too. Several designs are possible for a digestive system that doesn't let the flatlander fall to pieces. Some students might use a cul-de-sac approach to digestion, like that of an amoeba, in which food goes in and out the same opening. Others might interlock the two halves of the flatlander's body like pieces of a jigsaw puzzle. Still others might employ a linear digestive tract held together with little hooks, like Velcro: Only one pair of hooks opens at a time, so the flatlander stays intact. Enjoy the imaginative drawings you receive!

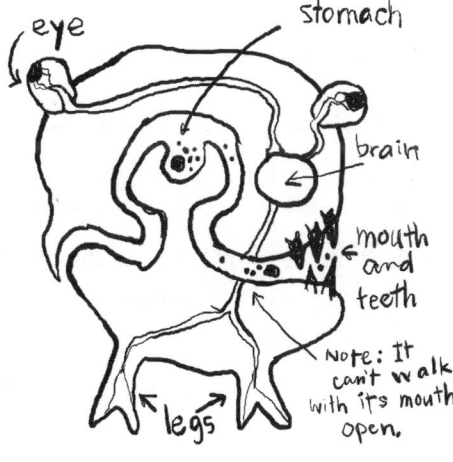

2.

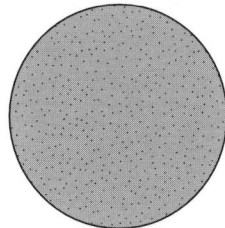

from above

from the side

Answers

3. For an image of a flatlander from three dimensions, see Question 1 (on the previous page). Flatlanders see a 1-dimensional image of their world. For example, the flatlander from Question 1 looks like this to her fellow flatlanders:

foot   mouth   eye   forehead

The line has a slight thickness for the benefit of human viewers. Flatlanders see a truly 1-dimensional line, with zero thickness.

Activity 2a: Coordinates

1.

Latitude	Longitude	City
23°30′ S	46°40′ W	São Paulo, Brazil
64°10′ N	21°50′ W	Reykjavik, Iceland
1°20′ S	36°50′ E	Nairobi, Kenya
22°30′ N	88°30′ E	Calcutta, India
21°20′ N	157°50′ W	Honolulu, Hawaii, USA
52°20′ N	4°50′ E	Amsterdam, Netherlands

2. A globe or world map should provide an estimate of your town's latitude and longitude. Answers accurate to the nearest degree are fine.

3. Students should realize that three coordinates serve to locate an object in space.

Bonus Problem

a. nearest: Lima, Peru

b. farthest: Bangkok, Thailand

   To find the location farthest away from a given point (the "antipodal point"), take the negative of the latitude (13° N instead of 13° S) and add 180° to the longitude (79° W + 180° = 101° E).

Answers

Activity 2b: Dimensions

1. One common method is to specify the airplane's latitude, longitude, and altitude. No matter what method is used, exactly three numbers are required.
2. Latitude and longitude suffice. Only two numbers are required.
3. The distance the train has traveled from Toronto completely specifies its location. Only one number is required.
4.
a.	your desktop	2-dimensional
b.	a straight line	1-dimensional
c.	the circumference of a circle	1-dimensional
d.	the inside of a circle	2-dimensional
e.	the surface of the moon	2-dimensional
f.	the inside of the moon	3-dimensional
g.	the surface of a doughnut	2-dimensional
h.	the surface of your skin	2-dimensional
i.	the air inside your classroom	3-dimensional
j.	a movie screen	2-dimensional
k.	the milk in a milk carton	3-dimensional

Bonus Problems

1. The number of seconds past midnight completely specifies the exact time on a given day. Only one number is required; therefore, time is 1-dimensional.
2. Three numbers are required to specify a color, for example, the intensities of the red, green, and blue light. Therefore, the set of all colors is 3-dimensional.

Activity 2c: Finite/Infinite, Boundary/No Boundary

1. a. infinite line: ∞ cm
      line segment with two endpoints: about 6 cm
      circumference of circle: about 6 cm
      ray: ∞ cm
      (Rough estimates are fine.)
   b. The only boundary points are the line segment's two endpoints and the ray's one endpoint.

Exploring the Shape of Space

Answers

   c. finite with boundary: line segment
      finite without boundary: circumference of a circle
      infinite with boundary: ray
      infinite without boundary: line

2. **a.** surface of sphere: about 12 cm^2
      interior of disk: about 4 cm^2
      infinite plane: ∞ cm^2
      half-infinite plane with edge: ∞ cm^2
      (Rough estimates are fine.)

   b. The only boundaries are the disk's circumference and the half-infinite plane's edge.

   c. finite with boundary: interior of disk
      finite without boundary: surface of sphere
      infinite with boundary: half-infinite plane
      infinite without boundary: infinite plane

Bonus Problem

Answers will vary. Here are some possibilities:
   finite with boundary: the space inside a room
   finite without boundary: the surface of a hypersphere or a 3-torus
      (This is the hard case. The 3-torus will be defined in Lesson 6.)
   infinite with boundary: a half-infinite 3-dimensional space, bounded
      by a plane
   infinite without boundary: infinite 3-dimensional space

Homework 2: Wraparound Universe

1. finite — Has a definite, limited length/area/volume.
   infinite — Has unlimited length/area/volume.
   boundary — Edge or border.
   1-dimensional — One number specifies a point.
   2-dimensional — Two numbers specify a point.
   3-dimensional — Three numbers specify a point.

2. 1-dimensional — Has length but no area.
   2-dimensional — Has area but no volume.
   3-dimensional — Has volume.

3. **a.** 2-dimensional (Two numbers specify a point, for example, latitude and longitude.)

   b. finite (It has a limited, measurable area.)

   c. No. (A flatlander could travel anywhere on the sphere's surface without ever encountering an edge.)

Answers

4. One example is an infinitely long strip of paper that has borders in two directions but extends to infinity in the other two directions.

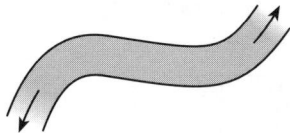

Bonus Problem

A linelander's skin consists of her two endpoints, which protect her insides from the outside air. The skin is 0-dimensional. It consists of a left endpoint and a right endpoint. No numbers are required to locate a point. By way of comparison, note that we 3-dimensional people have 2-dimensional skin, which protects our insides from the outside air. Similarly, the skin of a 2-dimensional flatlander is his 1-dimensional perimeter, where his body meets the air.

Activity 3a: Tic-Tac-Toe on a Cylinder

1. 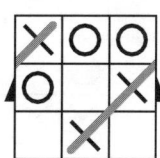   Neither player has won.

2. Look for sensible play, including a winning three-in-a-row in each game.

3.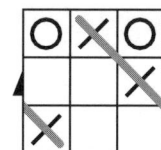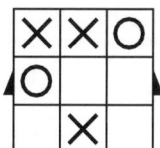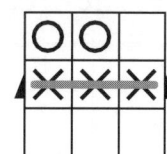

   In the third game, X cannot win immediately, so she must block O instead. If O then blocks X's potential win in the middle column, X wins with the middle right square instead.

Activity 3b: Equivalent Games

1. The first, second, and fourth are all equivalent.
   Second is equivalent to first (translate right).
   Third is equivalent to fifth.
   Fourth is equivalent to first (translate right then rotate 180°).
   Fifth is equivalent to third (translate right).

Answers

2. This chart shows each equivalent game as a combination of a reflection followed by a translation.

	No translation	Translate right	Translate left
No reflection	XX / OX / OO	XX / X O / O O	X X / OX / OO
Horizontal reflection	XX / XO / OO	X X / XO / OO	XX / O X / O O
Vertical reflection	OO / OX / XX	O O / X O / X X	OO / OX / X X
Horizontal and vertical reflections	OO / XO / XX	OO / XO / X X	O O / O X / XX

Note that a horizontal reflection plus a vertical reflection equals a 180° rotation.

Homework 3: Cylindrical Tic-Tac-Toe

1.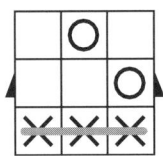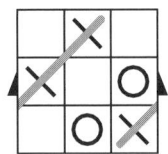

2. The first is equivalent to the second and third.
   The second is equivalent to the first (translate right).
   The third is equivalent to the first (rotate 180°, then translate left).
   The fourth is not equivalent to any other. (Columns a and b appear here, but the remaining column has the X in the wrong place.)

Answers

Bonus Problem

No. The first player (say X) can always win. Here's one strategy:

1. X makes her first move (anywhere!).
2. O makes his first move (anywhere!).
3. X makes a move threatening a win.
4. O is forced to block, but in doing so O threatens his own win.
5. X blocks O's potential win, and in doing so X creates *two* potential winning locations.
6. O can block only one of X's potential winning locations, so . . .
7. . . . X wins on her next move!

Super Bonus Problem

No. Surprisingly, every game of cylindrical tic-tac-toe must end in a win! Here's a proof. If the middle row contains all Xs or all Os, then somebody has won. Otherwise, it contains two Xs and one O, or vice versa. Without loss of generality, assume it is two Xs and one O. By translating if necessary, we may further assume that the O is in the middle, with an X on either side. If the middle column is all Os, then O has won. Otherwise, either the top middle or the bottom middle square contains an X. Without loss of generality, assume the top middle square contains an X. To keep X from winning, the bottom left and the bottom right squares must be Os. But that in turn forces the top left and top right squares to be Xs, giving a win for X across the top.

Homework 4: Torus Games

1.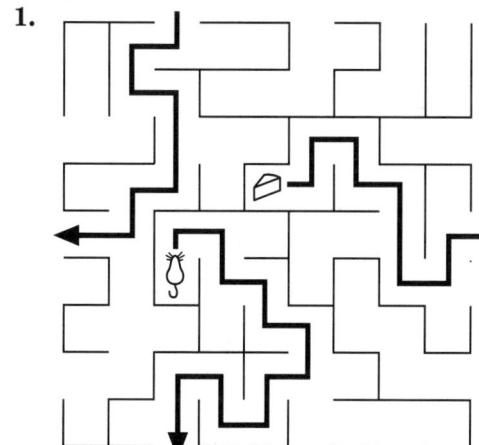

2.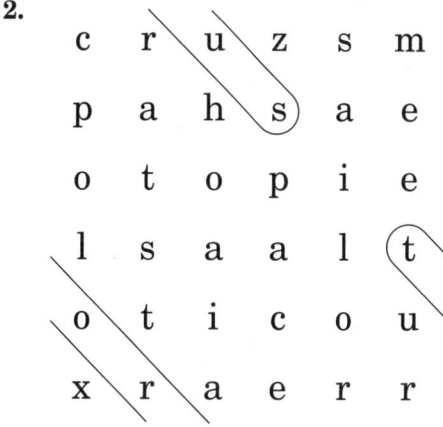

3. Finite, no boundary, 2-dimensional

Exploring the Shape of Space

Answers

4. a. She is still heading northeast.

b.

![diagram]

Bonus Problems

1. a. 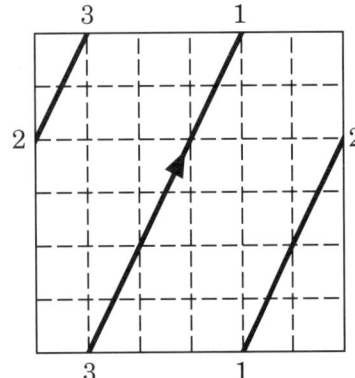   **b.**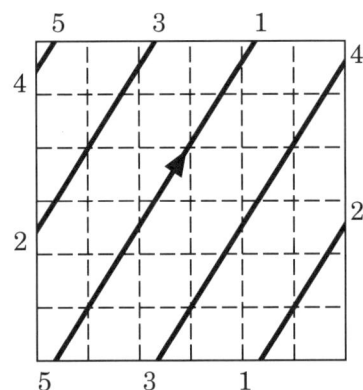

2. Answers will vary. Check that students' puzzles make essential use of the wraparound nature of the torus, both horizontally and vertically.

Activity 5: Games on a Torus

1.

2.

3. a. Red, blue, magenta, and yellow—all of them!

b. There is only one vine. It is very long.

4. a. 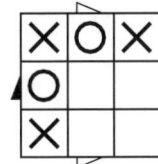   b.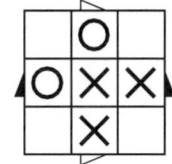

5. The first is directly equivalent (translate right and up to get the original), the second is not equivalent, and the third is equivalent by rotation (translate left and rotate).

Bonus Problems

1. The first move doesn't matter. Any first move is directly equivalent to any other.

2. The second player has two nonequivalent moves. To see why, first translate the board one unit down and one unit to the right, so the X appears in the center. It is now clear that the four squares immediately adjacent to the X are all equivalent to one another by 90° rotations, as are the four corner squares.

Homework 5: More Torus Games

1. They're all equivalent! To get to the first from the second, translate down and left; from the third, translate down and right; from the fourth, translate up and right; from the fifth, translate up and rotate 180°.

2. Typical fundamental domains are shown below. The important thing is that a fundamental domain contain each object in the universe exactly once. No object should be excluded, but none should appear twice.

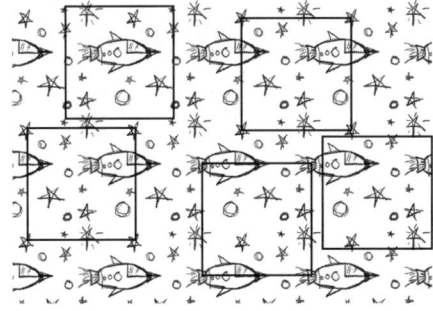

3. Each student's drawing will be different. The important points are that

   - the nine squares all have identical content
   - the design continue smoothly across the boundaries between squares, making creative use of the torus

Answers

Sample drawings:

Poor. The content is not the same in all nine squares, so this isn't a drawing on a torus.

Fair. This is a drawing on a torus, but the motif fails to use the torus's wraparound feature.

Good. The motif makes essential use of the torus. The part extending to the right interacts with the part extending to the left, and similarly up and down.

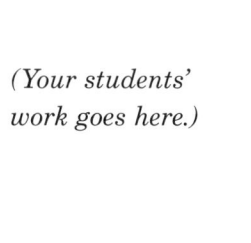

(Your students' work goes here.)

Excellent. The design is creative and expresses the student's special interests, as well as being correct as in the previous example.

4. A doughnut surface.

    Recall, though, that the doughnut surface is much less important in cosmology than the flat torus, as explained at the end of the teacher note for Lesson 4.

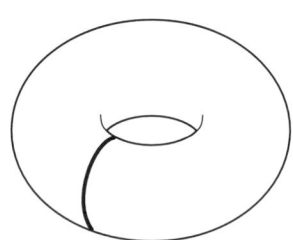

Bonus Problems

1. They're all equivalent! To discover how, focus on some easily recognizable feature, such as the curlicue in the center of the first maze. Then try to find the same feature (in this case, the curlicue) in each of the other mazes. You'll discover that it appears right side up in the second and third mazes, rotated 180° in the fourth maze, and reflected horizontally in the fifth. Once you've found it, check whether the remaining portions of the mazes match. This requires some care and patience!

2. The black queen moves three squares southwest to land just north of the white bishop, putting the white king in check. But wait—can the white knight capture the black queen? No; that would expose the white king to check by the black rook sitting three squares to his north. Checkmate!

Video Guide 1: The Shape of Space, Part 1

1. Cylinder, sphere, torus

2. The doughnut surface is cut open and deformed to a square. The resulting gluing diagram is identical to the flat torus the students studied in Lessons 4 and 5.

3. The video shows the flatlanders' 2-dimensional universe using only two dimensions as preparation for visualizing a finite 3-dimensional universe (the 3-torus) using only three dimensions. This saves students the trouble of learning to visualize 4-dimensional space.

4. The flatlanders can see the back of their own spaceship because their space wraps around and connects up with itself.

5. The humans can see the back of their own spaceship because their space connects up with itself.

6. Finite, no boundary

Activity 6a: The Real Universe

1. Answers will vary. The universe could be a 3-torus, although we still don't know one way or the other.

2. Answers will vary. For example, students might suggest sending a spaceship all the way around the universe (traveling in a straight line) or trying to see another image of ourselves.

3. Answers will vary, depending on the proposed experiments. For example, the universe is much too big to send a spaceship all the way around; even at the speed of light, a complete trip would take billions of years. And it would be difficult to recognize another image of our own Milky Way galaxy because we'd be seeing it as it was when it was much younger (and we don't know what it looks like from the outside even now).

Answers

Activity 6b: Torus Dimensions

1. a.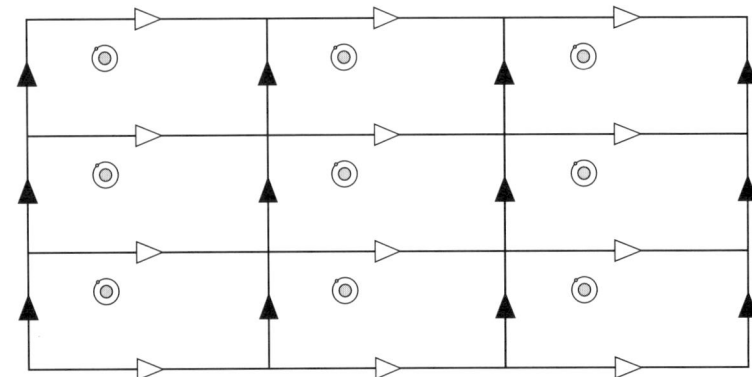

   b. There are two nearest images, one directly to the "north" and the other directly to the "south," because those are the directions in which their universe is narrowest.

   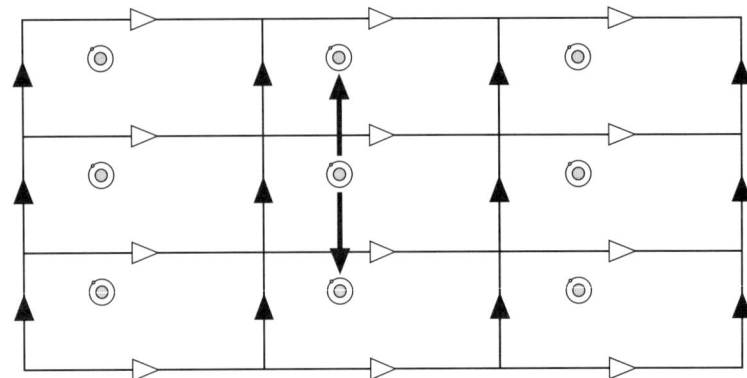

   c. 3 light-years

   d.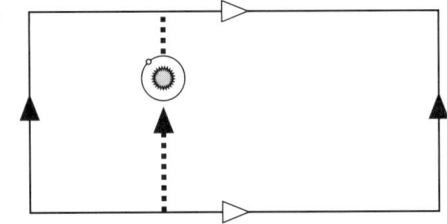

   The dotted line may be directed northward, southward, in both directions, or in neither.

   e. They see their solar system as it was three years earlier, on Csir 17, 3506, because it takes the light three years to reach them. In other words, the light they observe spends three years circumnavigating the universe before returning to the solar system from which it started.

2. a. We would see our nearest images in the direction in which the universe is narrowest, that is, to the left or right in the picture.

b. 150 million light-years

c.

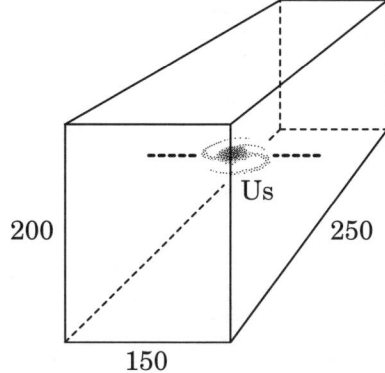

d. The humans see the Milky Way as it was 150 million years ago.

(Note: This answer is correct in a static universe, but in reality the humans would see the Milky Way as it was somewhat *less* than 150 million years ago. The reason is that the real universe is expanding, so during the early portions of its trip, the light was traversing a universe smaller than the present one and therefore making better progress than it otherwise would have.)

Bonus Problem

Mirrors on opposite walls give infinitely many images of everything in the room.

The images in the mirrored room and in the 3-torus are similar in that each shows infinitely many images of every object. The images differ in two ways:

- In the mirrored room, alternate images are reversed. For example, alternate images of a person face forward and backward. In a 3-torus, all images face the same direction. Thus, for example, if the person takes a step forward, pairs of images get closer to each other in the mirrored room (ultimately meeting at the mirror), but in the 3-torus they stay the same distance apart.

  Older students, already familiar with the concepts of translation, rotation, and reflection, may observe that neighboring images in the mirrored room differ by reflection, while neighboring images in the 3-torus differ by translation.

- In the mirrored room, the images repeat in only one dimension. In the 3-torus, they repeat in all dimensions. If the room's floor, ceiling, and all four walls were covered with mirrors, this difference would be eliminated.

Exploring the Shape of Space

Answers

Homework 6: The 3-Torus

1. Finite, no boundary, 3-dimensional
2. Square; triangle; hexagon; trapezoid
3. Cube; sphere; sphere; cone
4. 300 meters (parallel to the block's shortest edges)

Bonus Problem

Choose the fundamental domain so that its corner is at space station A. Place the other space station, B, at the very center of the fundamental domain.

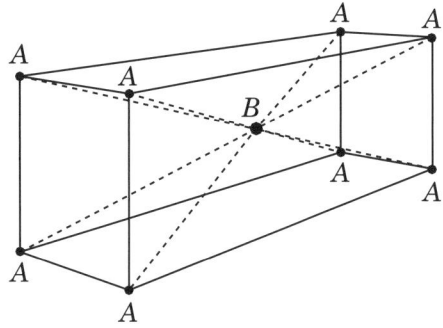

Super Bonus Problem

1300 km. First apply the Pythagorean theorem as $300^2 + 400^2 = 500^2$ to solve for the distance $d = 500$ km from the center of the box to the midpoint of an edge. Then apply it again as $500^2 + 1200^2 = 1300^2$ to solve for the desired distance $D = 1300$ km from one space station to the other.

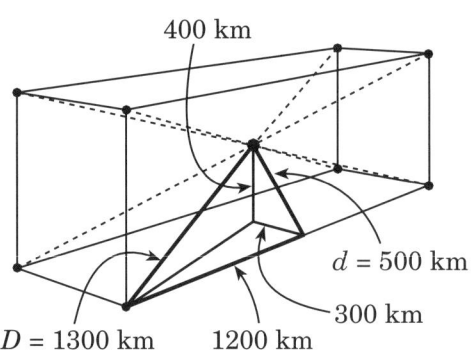

Reading: Cosmology

1. Infinite
2. Finite; yes
3. Like Aristotle, Europeans before A.D. 1600 thought of the universe as finite, with a spherical boundary, and Earth at its center.
4. The discovery that different stars lie at different distances from Earth, some beyond Aristotle's boundary sphere
5. Georg Riemann. He proposed the hypersphere, the 3-dimensional surface of a 4-dimensional ball.
6. The 3-torus
7. A galaxy is a cluster of stars.
8. We live in the Milky Way. Our galaxy got that name because it looks like milk spilled across the sky.
9. With the naked eye we can see one other galaxy (Andromeda). With the Hubble Space Telescope we can see roughly one hundred billion (100,000,000,000) galaxies.

Answers

10. Alexander Friedmann

11. We know space is expanding because of the red shift; the light from distant stars is "stretched out."

12. The universe is approximately 15 billion (15,000,000,000) years old.

13. For its first 300,000 years, the whole universe was filled with a material similar to the outer layers of the modern sun. (The material was a plasma consisting of ions, electrons, and radiation.)

14. The light was stretched out by the expansion of space.

15. Fossils are to paleontology as <u>the microwave background radiation</u> is to cosmology.

Activity 7a: Making Möbius Strips

2. The line must go around the Möbius strip twice before returning to the X; the Möbius strip has only one side! The line on the cylinder goes around only once; the cylinder has two sides.

3.
Möbius strip

4.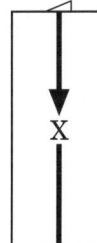

5. A Möbius strip has only one boundary circle. (The ant passes point B before returning to point A.)

6. **a.** The Möbius strip stays connected! You get only one piece, a cylinder with twists in it.

   b. This time the strip comes apart. You get two linked cylinders, each with two twists.

Activity 7b: Möbius Strip Tiling View

1. **a.** The Möbius strip wraps around and connects up with itself in the vertical direction. Flatlanders living in it would see repeating images of themselves to the north and south. The Möbius strip has a boundary along its side. Flatlanders looking to the west or east would see nothing, because their universe stops at the boundary.

Exploring the Shape of Space

Answers

b. The top of the fundamental domain is glued to the bottom with a flip (a half twist). Thus, in the tiling view, each copy of the fundamental domain is the mirror image of its neighbors.

2. a. 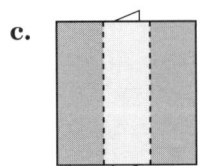 Student games will vary.

   b. Check that each student's fundamental domain has been copied accurately into the tiling view. Every other copy should be identical to the original fundamental domain, while the alternate copies are reversed side to side.

3. In each game, check that the moves are consistent. That is, whenever an X or O appears in one copy of the fundamental domain, it should appear in all copies. Most important, alternate images should be reversed side to side.

Bonus Problem

This game is played exactly as in Question 3 above, in spite of the conceptual leap of erasing the seam. Check that students' moves are consistent; that is, each row should be identical to the row three units above or below it but reversed side to side.

Homework 7: Möbius Strips

1. a. All answers are acceptable. Look for predictions of number of pieces, length of pieces, and number of twists in each piece.

   b. There are two connected loops. One loop is a Möbius strip, as long as the original but only a third as wide. The other loop is a cylinder that is twice as long as the original Möbius strip and has two full twists.

   c. The two outer thirds combine to form the twisted cylinder, while the middle third forms the $\frac{1}{3}$-width Möbius strip.

122   Exploring the Shape of Space

Answers

2. 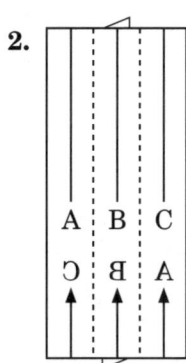 Bobbie (B) returns to her starting position first. Alex and Chris arrive at each other's starting positions after their first lap around the track and must run a second lap to arrive back at their own starting positions.

(Note: Bobbie would be on the wrong side of a paper Möbius strip after only one trip around, but this problem doesn't occur in a virtual Möbius strip, which is a purely 2-dimensional world and doesn't have a "top surface" or "bottom surface" as the paper Möbius strip does. When reviewing this homework problem, you may want to illustrate the race on a clear plastic Möbius strip made from a transparency.)

Bonus Problem

Yes. They both lie on an edge. If you translate the Möbius strip on the left two units upward, it will look like the one on the right (because of the flip in the Möbius strip).

Activity 8: Games on a Klein Bottle

1. a. 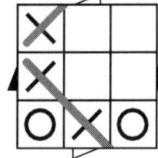 **b.**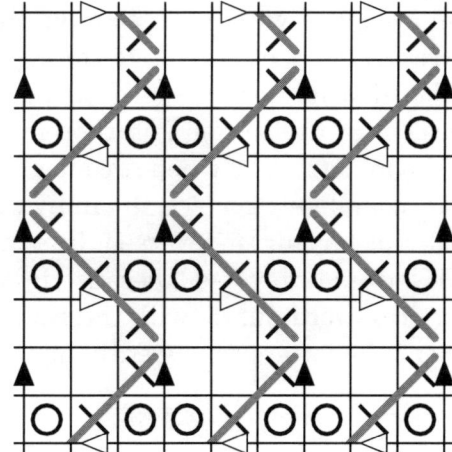

2. a. His tail used to curl to the left, but now it curls to the right. This happens because the board's top and bottom are glued with a flip.

b. No. He still looks the same.

c. Anything that leaves the top of the board some distance to the left of a dotted green line returns at the bottom the same distance to the right of the line, and vice versa. The dotted green lines are the ***glide reflection axes.*** Older students may already have seen glide reflections in their previous study of symmetry.

Exploring the Shape of Space

Answers

3. a. Yes or no. Depending on how they assemble the puzzle, some students will find that the piece fits, while others will find it to be the mirror image of what's required.

b. No or yes. The piece is now the mirror image of what it used to be, so students who answered yes to 3a should answer no here, and vice versa.

c. Yes or no. The piece would have traveled around the board an even number of times (the first time plus 4317 more times equals 4318 times altogether), so it would be back to its original self. Therefore, this answer should be the same as the answer to 3a and the opposite of the answer to 3b.

4. a.

			e		
		r			
	t				
			a		
				l	
b					

b.

		e			
			r		
				t	
			a		
					l
b					

c. The board's top and bottom are glued with a flip, so anything crossing them gets mirror-reversed. Another way to think of it is that if the name "Albert" is slanting toward the dotted green symmetry axis when it goes out at the bottom left, then it must still be slanting toward the symmetry axis when it comes back in at the top right. (Note: To be completely correct, the individual letters *e*, *r*, and *t* would each appear mirror-reversed. But the computer game displays all letters unreversed, because in a Klein bottle word search or crossword puzzle with interlocking words it's impossible to orient the letters consistently in all words at once.)

d.

		i	e		
		s	r		
		t			
		o	c		
		p	h		
		h	r		

e. It can't fit in a 6-by-6 torus without overlapping itself.

Answers

Homework 8: Klein Bottle Games

1. X can win in *any* square of the bottom row.

2. Answers will vary. The best puzzles will include words that wrap around horizontally, words that wrap around vertically, several long words (seven letters or more), and a large number of intersecting words.

3. a. Just to the right of the symmetry line at the bottom

   b. Just to the left of the symmetry line at the bottom

   c. Exactly on the symmetry line (but mirror-reversed)

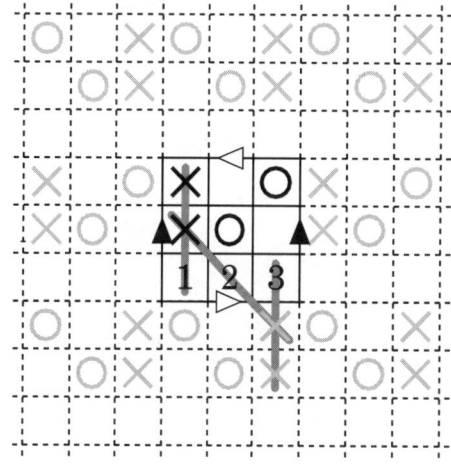

4.

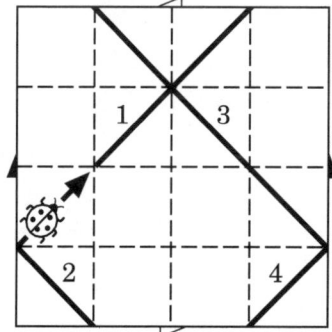

Bonus Problems

1. Answers will vary. Check that each puzzle is doable and that words reflect correctly as they pass across the top/bottom of the fundamental domain.

2. Answers will vary. As in Homework 5, Question 2, the important thing is that a fundamental domain contains each object in the universe exactly once. If a student uses a rectangular fundamental domain, it's best for the vertical sides to align with the Klein bottle's symmetry axes (as in the second "good" domain at right) so that the top and bottom edges match nicely. If the vertical sides don't align with the symmetry axes (as in the "fair" domain), then the top and bottom edges will disagree with each other and can't be glued in the usual Klein bottle way.

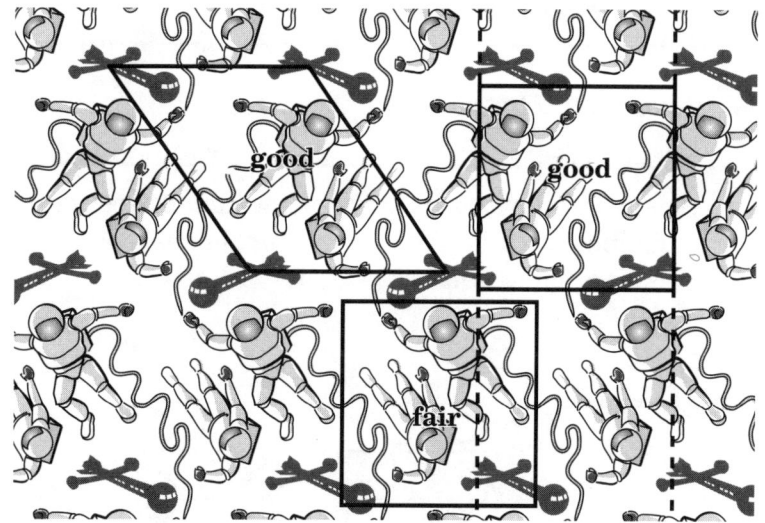

Exploring the Shape of Space

Answers

3. Yes. In a 5-by-5 Klein bottle a single letter may appear more than once in the same word (see *visualize* below left), but in a 6-by-6 Klein bottle the word passes through itself without overlap (see *imagination* below right).

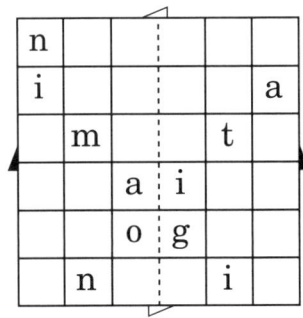

Video Guide 2: The Shape of Space, Part 2

1. Finite
2. No boundary
3. Yes; if some of their images are reversed, they are in a Klein space.
4. Yes

Activity 9: Mystery Spaces

Mystery Space 1	quarter-turn space
Mystery Space 2	3-torus
Mystery Space 3	half-turn space
Mystery Space 4	Klein space

Homework 9: More Shapes for Space

1. Klein space; quarter-turn space; 3-torus; half-turn space
2. Answers will vary. For example, we might see some peculiar combination of galaxies in one part of space and then see the same combination in another part, only rotated 90°.

Test

1. [12 points]

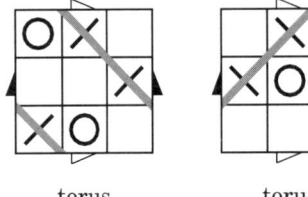 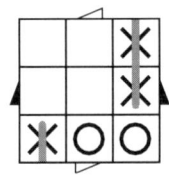 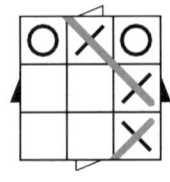

126

Exploring the Shape of Space

Answers

2. [12 points]

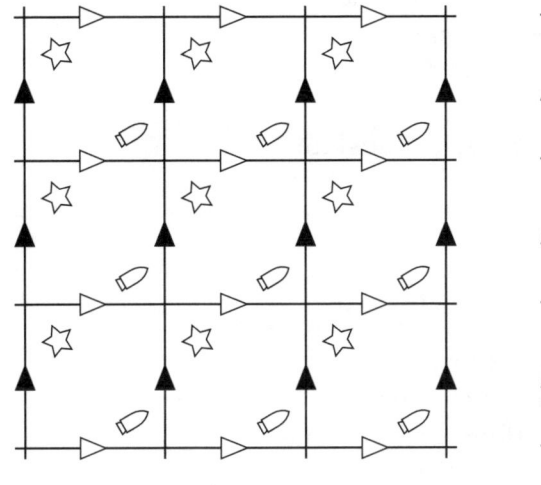
torus

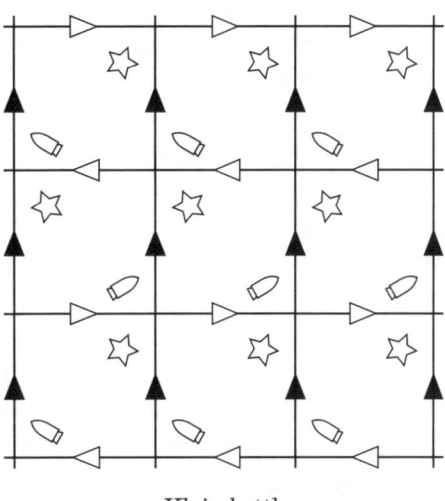
Klein bottle

3. [10 points]

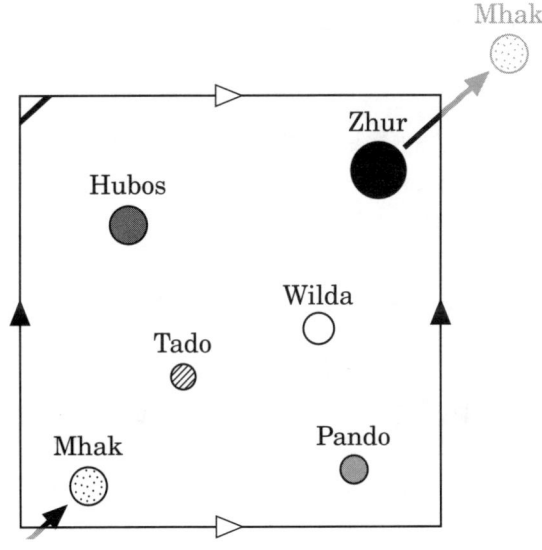

4. [12 points]

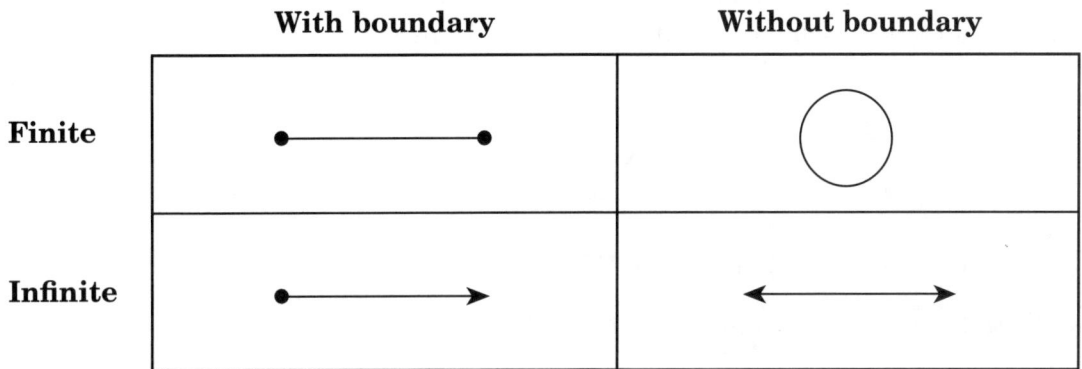

Exploring the Shape of Space

Answers

5. [10 points]

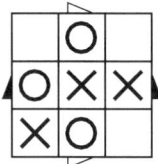

The fourth game is not equivalent to the others because two Os appear in the same column. The rest are equivalent. To get to the first from the second, translate down; from the third, reflect across the diagonal line of Os and then translate up; from the fifth, translate left.

6. [6 points]

Finite; no boundary; 3-dimensional

7. [5 points]

Answers will vary. Some students may say that a 2-torus is constructed from a square while a 3-torus is constructed from a cube. Others may point out that the 2-torus is 2-dimensional while the 3-torus is 3-dimensional.

8. [10 points]

Yes. If our universe is a 3-torus, we might be able to see the same galaxy in two different directions, because there's more than one way for its light to reach us.

9. [5 points]

To make a Möbius strip, glue the ends of a paper strip with a half twist. To make a cylinder, glue the ends of a paper strip with no twist.

10. [8 points]

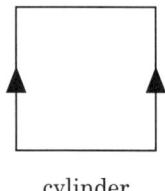 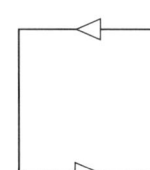 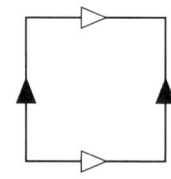 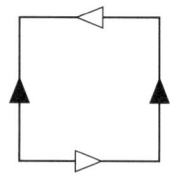

cylinder　　　　Möbius strip　　　　torus　　　　Klein bottle

11. [10 points]

Answers will vary. The important thing is that students draw true 2-dimensional flatlanders and houses, not 2-dimensional images of 3-dimensional houses. Compare to the Homework 1 answers.

good　　　　　　　　bad

Glossary

1-dimensional — Only one number is required to specify a location; has length but no area. A line and the circumference of a circle are examples of 1-dimensional spaces.

2-dimensional — Two numbers are required to specify a location; has area but no volume. A plane and the surface of a sphere are examples of 2-dimensional spaces.

3-dimensional — Three numbers are required to specify a location; has volume. Standard Euclidean space, a solid ball, and the 3-torus are all examples of 3-dimensional spaces.

2-torus — See *torus*.

3-torus — See *torus*.

boundary — An edge of space. A traveler who reaches a boundary can go no farther. The boundary of a line segment is its endpoints, the boundary of a square is its perimeter, and the boundary of a solid ball is its spherical surface. Some spaces, such as (infinite) Euclidean space or a (finite) torus, have no boundary.

cosmology — The study of the universe as a whole.

cylinder — A tube. To construct a cylinder, take a rectangular piece of paper and glue together one pair of opposite edges.

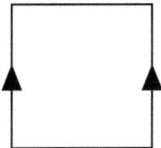 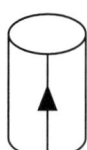

Exploring the Shape of Space

Glossary (continued)

equivalent gluing diagrams Two gluing diagrams are equivalent if they define the same object. For example, the two gluing diagrams shown here are equivalent because they give the same tic-tac-toe game on a cylinder. To see this more directly, copy each diagram onto a sheet of paper, roll the sheets into cylinders, and compare—they will be identical.

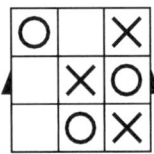 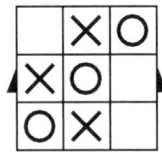

finite Has a limited, measurable length/area/volume. (Antonym: *infinite*)

fundamental domain A region used to construct a space. For example, a square is a fundamental domain for a 2-torus, and a cube is a fundamental domain for a 3-torus.

glide reflection A reflection followed by a translation. The dotted line in the figure is the glide reflection axis.

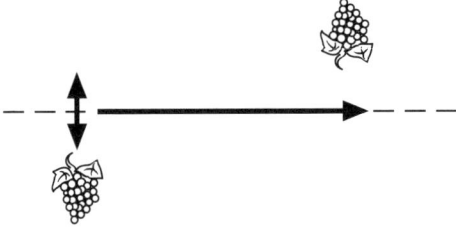

gluing diagram A polygon with marks indicating how the sides are to be glued. For example, the gluing diagram for a torus, shown here, is a square with arrows showing that opposite sides are to be glued straight across, without twisting. A gluing diagram for a 3-dimensional space is a polyhedron, with markings showing how the faces are to be glued.

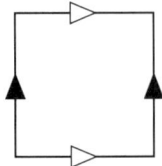

130

Exploring the Shape of Space
©2001 Key Curriculum Press

Glossary (continued)

half-turn space   A cubical block of space with two pairs of faces glued straight across (as in a 3-torus) but the third pair of faces glued with a half-turn.

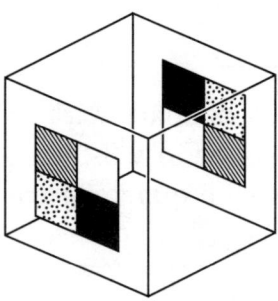

infinite   Has unlimited length/area/volume. (Antonym: *finite*)

Klein bottle   The gluing diagram for a Klein bottle, shown here, is a square with one pair of opposite sides glued straight across (as in a cylinder) and the other pair glued with a flip (as in a Möbius strip).

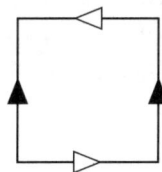

Klein space   A cubical block of space with two pairs of faces glued straight across (as in a 3-torus) but the third pair of faces glued with a flip. Each horizontal slice of the 3-dimensional Klein space is a 2-dimensional Klein bottle.

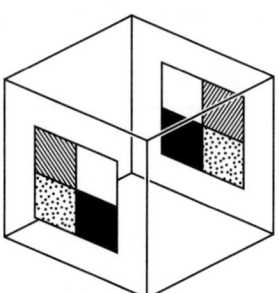

Glossary (continued)

Möbius strip A rectangle with one pair of opposite sides glued with a flip.

quarter-turn space A cubical block of space with two pairs of faces glued straight across (as in a 3-torus) but the third pair of faces glued with a quarter-turn.

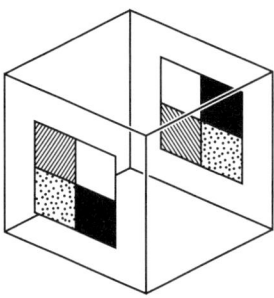

reflection In two dimensions a reflection holds a line still while interchanging the half planes to either side of it. In three dimensions a reflection holds a plane still while interchanging the half spaces to either side of it.

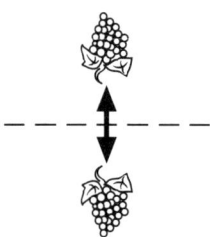

rotation A rotation holds one point of an object or space still and moves the object or space around that point.

Glossary (continued)

tiling view An infinite lattice of repeating images showing the contents of a finite space over and over. The tiling view corresponds to what an inhabitant of the finite space would see as he or she looked around.

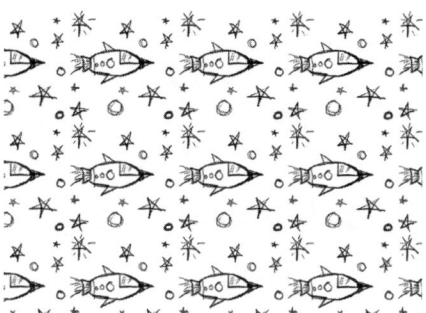

torus A *2-dimensional torus* (or *2-torus*) is a square with both pairs of opposite sides glued straight across, with no flip.

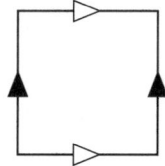

A *3-dimensional torus* (or *3-torus*) is a cube with all three pairs of opposite faces glued straight across, with no twisting.

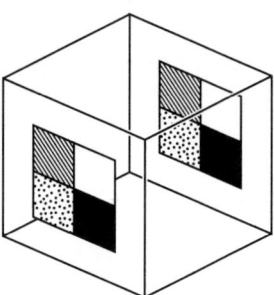

translation A translation moves an object or space in a fixed direction, without rotation or reflection.